LIFE IN THE THIR[...]

LIFE IN THE THIRD REICH

Edited, with an Introduction, by

RICHARD BESSEL

Oxford   New York

OXFORD UNIVERSITY PRESS

1987

Oxford University Press, Walton Street, Oxford OX2 6DP

Oxford New York Toronto
Delhi Bombay Calcutta Madras Karachi
Petaling Jaya Singapore Hong Kong Tokyo
Nairobi Dar es Salaam Cape Town
Melbourne Auckland

and associated companies in
Beirut Berlin Ibadan Nicosia

Oxford is a trade mark of Oxford University Press

These articles were first published in History Today between October 1985
and February 1986
First issued, with a new introduction, as an Oxford University paperback, and
simultaneously in a hardback edition, 1987

British Library Cataloguing in Publication Data
Life in the Third Reich.
1. Germany—History—1933–1945
I. Bessel, Richard
943.086 DD256.5
ISBN 0–19–215892–9
ISBN 0–19–285184–5 Pbk

Library of Congress Cataloging in Publication Data
Life in the Third Reich.
"First published in History today between October 1985 and February 1986"—T.p. verso.
Bibliography: p. Includes index.
1. Germany—Social life and customs—20th century. 2. Germany—Social
conditions—1933–1945. 3. National socialism. I. Bessel, Richard.
DD256.5.L52 1987 943.086 87–5518
ISBN 0–19–215892–9
ISBN 0–19–285184–5 (pbk.)

Set by Colset Private Ltd.
Printed in Great Britain by
Richard Clay Ltd,
Bungay, Suffolk

PREFACE

THIS book contains eight essays originally published between October 1985 and February 1986 in *History Today*, together with an extended introduction. I would like to offer my special thanks to the people who helped make this book possible: Sabine Phillips, who typed the original manuscript; Richard Deveson, who translated the articles by Detlev Peukert and Ulrich Herbert from the German; Gordon Marsden, the present editor of *History Today*; Juliet Gardiner, the previous editor of *History Today*, who originally commissioned the articles and whose careful editorial eye was indispensable in putting them together; and Jacqueline Guy, Art and Production Editor of *History Today*, for her tremendous efforts in gathering the illustrations.

RICHARD BESSEL

CONTENTS

ABBREVIATIONS

BDM	*Bund Deutscher Mädel*, League of German Girls
Gestapo	*Geheime Staatspolizei*, Secret State Police
KPD	*Kommunistische Partei Deutschlands*, Communist Party of Germany
NSDAP	*Nationalsozialistische Deutsche Arbeiterpartei*, National Socialist German Workers Party
OKW	*Oberkommando der Wehrmacht*, Military High Command
SA	*Sturmabteilungen*, Storm Sections
SD	*Sicherheitsdienst*, Security Service
SPD	*Sozialdemokratische Partei Deutschlands*, Social Democratic Party of Germany
SS	*Schutzstaffel*, Protection Squads

LIST OF ILLUSTRATIONS

INTRODUCTION

Richard Bessel

FEW historical subjects are so emotive as the Third Reich, and few have stimulated so much general interest. The reasons for this are many: the Nazi regime unleashed the most destructive war in the history of the modern world, laying waste to much of the European continent and, through Germany's defeat, ensuring the dominance of the superpowers in European affairs. Its flamboyant, theatrical style of politics—immortalised through contemporary newsreels (which had reached a level of considerable technical sophistication, not least with sound recording, during the 1930s)—continues to fascinate and to horrify. Its creator and leader, Adolf Hitler, still commands widespread interest—despite the efforts of historians who prefer to stress impersonal, structural factors than to focus on the role of personality in politics. And its sheer barbaric criminality—culminating in the murder of millions of innocent human beings during the Second World War—remains one of the central historical problems of our time. The Nazi regime fortunately is dead and buried, but the questions raised by its terrible history continue to demand explanations.

The main outlines of the history of Nazi Germany are well known: the collapse of Weimar democracy, the rise of Hitler, the erection of a brutal dictatorship, rearmament, the launching of the Second World War, the persecution and mass murder of European Jews, the total defeat of the German Reich. Few, if any, regimes have been subjected to such close scrutiny, not least because Germany's defeat left its governmental records available to historians remarkably quickly. Yet in the past few years the interests of many students of modern Germany have gone beyond the familiar contours of that country's recent political history. The revolution which has taken place in the historical profession in recent years has brought new perspectives to analyses of the Nazi regime. Local and regional studies, examinations of social questions, and investigations into how people lived their everyday lives have done much to enrich our understanding of the 'course of German history'. There has been a growing awareness of the interconnections between the major political decisions in the Third Reich and what was happening on the ground; historians of Nazi Germany have at last discovered the German people.

This shift in emphasis is due not just to current fashion among social historians. More than forty years now have elapsed since the Third Reich came crashing down. Much archive material, particularly at local and regional level, has become readily accessible only recently. Perhaps more importantly, although the period is still close enough to allow us to question those who lived through it, enough time now has elapsed for such questioning to have lost many of the accusatory overtones which marked discussions twenty years ago about the nature of fascism and the responsibility of the older generation for the crimes of National Socialism. The issues presented by the history of Nazi Germany are no less highly charged today than they ever have been, but we now are able to grapple with them in ways which two decades ago would have been difficult, if not impossible.

One particularly telling indication of this is the recent essay competition among German school pupils (the 'Schülerwettbewerb Deutsche Geschichte' sponsored by the Körber–Stiftung) on the subject of 'Daily Life under National Socialism', a competition which attracted tens of thousands of entrants. After the competition was announced in 1981, municipal archives in the Federal Republic were inundated with teenagers examining local newspapers and administrative records from the 1930s. Some of the projects were individual efforts, some the efforts of small groups, others the products of entire school classes. Pupils investigated such subjects as the history of their own schools during the Nazi period, life in concentration camps, the persecution of the Jewish minority in their communities, struggles in the local Church organisations, the impact of the Hitler Youth, working-class resistance; and a number of the studies developed into quite sophisticated and informative articles, which were published during the following year.* It would have been difficult to imagine such activity —the public questioning of the generation which lived through the Third Reich by their descendents, in order to discover and analyse rather than to accuse—twenty years earlier. The resonance of this competition and the quality of the work it stimulated say a great deal about contemporary Germany's changing relation to her recent past.

The upsurge of interest in social history, in local history, in the ways in which people actually lived their lives during the Nazi period, has altered the ways in which many historians now view the Third Reich. To be sure, this new interest brings with it the danger of getting lost in the minutiae of day-to-day life in one local community after another—of a narrow antiquarianism and a myopic concentration on 'ordinary' concerns, losing sight of the fact that the Third Reich was in a perpetual state of emergency and that people's everyday experiences were shaped by a political system which murdered millions of people. In short, there is a danger of trivialising the subject, and accusations that historians trivialise their subject have a particularly bitter ring when that subject is Nazi Germany. Thus it is all the more necessary that these new perspectives on Nazi Germany be used to open up the larger questions, that we both appreciate the complexity of the structures of people's lives and maintain clear analytical goals when examining these structures.

When approached in this way, these new emphases promise greatly to broaden our understanding of recent German

* Dieter Galinski, Ulrich Herbert and Ulla Lachauer (eds.), *Nazis und Nachbarn. Schüler erforschen den Alltag im Nationalsozialismus* (Hamburg, 1982).

history. The early focus on Hitler and Nazi politics as seen from government offices in Berlin (or from Nazi Party headquarters in Munich) no longer is sufficient. No longer is it possible to regard the horrific history of Nazi Germany as the product of a few demonic politicians (or even more pointedly, 'the will of a single madman') who entranced millions of Germans and sent them down a path towards war and mass murder. Questions, for example, about how it was possible for the Nazi regime to embark upon the extermination of European Jewry no longer can be limited to examination of Nazi ideology, the stated intentions of certain Nazi politicians and the grizzly chronology of the destruction of millions of innocent lives: for we now know a great deal about not only the mechanics of decision-making in the Nazi system, but also about the nature of popular support for the regime and the role of anti-Semitism in generating that support. No longer is our picture of popular attitudes towards the Third Reich so framed by the propaganda images skillfully generated under the watchful eye of Goebbels's Propaganda Ministry; increasingly it has been possible to get behind the propaganda façade created by the Nazi regime, to examine the extremely paradoxical nature of life in the Third Reich. Understandably with the history of Nazi Germany it has been particularly tempting to paint pictures in stark black and white, clearly delineating categories of good and evil—for was not the Third Reich the most thoroughly evil political system ever created? But life is not like that. Human beings are bundles of paradoxes, and the choices they are forced to make rarely are clearcut. In order to understand the mechanics of politics and the social history of the Third Reich, it is necessary to appreciate that even under Hitler everyday life was characterised by contradiction and paradox.

Some revealing examples of this may be found in the areas of morality and 'law and order'. As we all know too well, the Nazi regime was perhaps the most criminal, barbarous, and immoral that the world has ever seen. However, it also was a regime which made great—and successful—efforts to present itself as the defender of conventional social and moral values, as the guarantor of public decency and of law and order. Indeed, the Nazi regime appeared to offer a remarkably effective 'law and order' government. Until the war created new tensions, the Nazi state was quite successful in its campaign against ordinary crime; in the years after the Nazis came to power, the recorded incidence of most categories of serious crime registered sharp falls. Although such crime statistics are notoriously problematic, comments one still hears in Germany about how 'under Adolf' it was safe to walk the streets bear witness to the positive and durable impression made upon the respectable citizenry by the Nazi drive against crime. Similarly, the Nazi State made considerable and successful attempts to suppress the production and distribution of pornographic literature; tough police and customs measures, combined with the growing difficulties Germans had in acquiring the foreign currency necessary to buy pornography from abroad, were very effective. A parallel campaign was conducted against prostitution; no sooner had the Nazis come to power than they proceeded to arrest thousands of prostitutes in an attempt to 'clean up the streets'. Such campaigns certainly appealed to a broad desire for 'decency' in public life.

Yet at the same time the Nazis' own propaganda sometimes bordered on the pornographic; brothels were set up during the war for German soldiers, for foreign labourers, and in concentration camps; and the Nazi government itself and its police forces effectively destroyed the rule of law (with regard to people, if not with regard to property). On the one hand, the Nazi regime gained widespread popular support as an effective law and order government; on the other, it was a regime in which the activities of the Secret State Police (Gestapo) were not subject to review by the administrative courts and whose 'Chief of German Police' (Heinrich Himmler) could write in 1937 that in his view 'the police, like the Wehrmacht, can act only according to the orders of its leadership and not according to laws'.

The contradictory and paradoxical nature of life in the Third Reich emerges most clearly when historical investigation focuses not just on 'high politics' but also on the experience of people living under the Nazi regime. The decisions people had to make, the opinions they expressed, and thus their input into the politics of the day were rarely straightforward, nor should we expect that they should be so. The day-to-day reality of the Third Reich involved a complex mixture of fear and bribery, of terror and concessions, of barbarism and appeals to conventional moral values, which were employed in order to gain and maintain a grip on German society. Immense difficulties arise in trying to make sense of this mixture, not least because these contradictory mechanisms came into play simultaneously. But this does not mean that the difficulties should be side-stepped. An understanding of the history of the Third Reich, and the wider implications that it has for understanding other societies, lies precisely in trying to make sense of a society in which people who may have despised Nazi Party bosses, feared Gestapo agents in their factories, felt aggrieved by the government's attempts to hold down their wages, and certainly did not want to go to war, might at the same time have felt pleased that Germany could force the incorporation of Austria and the Sudetenland into the Reich, be grateful that they were back at work after years of unemployment, or be extremely impressed by the holiday programmes offered by the 'Strength through Joy' organisation.

When we begin to investigate the Third Reich at this level, to examine the ways in which 'ordinary' human beings lived through these years, the all-too-familiar history of Nazi Germany begins often to emerge in a new light. What may appear to be a quite extraordinary regime when the main focus is the 'Führer' often looks rather different when the objects of discussion are the everyday experiences of Germans living under Nazi rule. Were, for example, the ways in which the Nazi regime tried to secure popular legitimation all that different from the ways in which other regimes have attempted this at other times? Was the behaviour of Germans in the often awful situations created by the Nazi regime of a fundamentally different nature from the behaviour of other people at other times and in other places? Is it right to separate out the tortured history of Nazi Germany as something quite unique? All too often discussion of Nazi Germany stops dead, with its leader in the Berlin bunker, in 1945; yet since most of the people who experienced the Nazi regime survived it, were not their experiences of fundamental importance in shaping the ways in which they viewed (and acted in) the world subsequently? This is not to assert that a regime which unleashed a world war and murdered millions of people in cold blood was no different from any other political regime. It is, however, to suggest that perhaps the history of Nazi Germany might have more to tell us about society and politics elsewhere than many people would like to admit.

The difficulties involved in coming to terms with the many paradoxes thrown up by the history of the Third Reich, as well as in making sense of a complex economic structure and an even more complex political system, no doubt have helped to create a disturbing gap between popular perceptions of Nazi Germany and the concerns of many historians. Despite the tremendous interest in, and literature on, the Third Reich, no doubt many people would be surprised, for example, to learn that historians have found little evidence of active support among Germans for anti-Semitic atrocities during the 1930s or 1940s; that the Autobahns were not essentially a product of a vast rearmament programme favoured by the military; that historians generally regard the great 'totalitarian' Nazi State not as a well-oiled machine but a chaotic and stunningly inefficient political system in which competing organisations were engaged in a desperate struggle to expand their influence and power at each other's expense; or that one leading historian of Nazi Germany (Hans Mommsen) has gone so far as to describe Hitler as a 'weak dictator'. No doubt the historical profession itself is partly to blame: difficult prose (embedded in expensive monographs) about structural factors determining the shape and trajectory of the Third Reich can hardly be expected to capture the popular imagination. Simpler, if not terribly accurate, explanations are altogether better suited to television documentaries which depend upon available newsreel footage and which shape so much of historical consciousness in the contemporary world. Perhaps Goebbels's propaganda continues to have a greater effect in shaping popularly held images of the Third Reich than we would like to think.

This book represents an attempt to redress the balance: to reduce the gap between recent historical research and widely held pictures of Nazi Germany and, at the same time, to present in an accessible form some new perspectives on the paradoxical nature of life in the Third Reich. As a consequence of the explosion of research into the social and political history of modern Germany, we now can see many familiar (and many not so familiar) themes in the history of Nazi Germany in a new light. The articles presented in this book offer glimpses of some of the new approaches developed in recent years. In some cases the subjects themselves may be familiar, even if their treatment is not: the role of political violence in bringing the Nazis to power; the nature of the Nazi State; Nazi policy against the Jews; how Hitler was regarded by the German people. In other cases they are less familiar: the nature of village society, and the changes it underwent, during the course of the Third Reich; the treatment of 'social outcasts' such as gypsies or Germans regarded as 'asocial'; youth culture and youth gangs in Nazi Germany; the ways in which Germans regarded their own experience under Hitler in retrospect. This volume obviously cannot provide a comprehensive social history of Nazi Germany: many important topics are, unfortunately, missing—for example, life in the armed forces (which comprised a large proportion of the daily lives of many Germans during the short history of the 'Thousand-Year Reich') or the social role of the

churches. Nor is it an attempt to offer a single unified interpretation (by a new historical 'school') of the history of the
Third Reich: the authors come from diverse backgrounds—
teaching in Britain, the Federal Republic of Germany, and the
United States—and approach their subjects in a variety of ways.
In many respects this collection provides more new questions
than answers. But all the contributions aim to bring new perspectives to bear on some of the most challenging problems
which confront the historian of the modern world, and offer to
a wider public some of the fruits of new research on Nazi
Germany.

POLITICAL VIOLENCE AND THE NAZI SEIZURE OF POWER

Richard Bessel

MANY contemporary observers of the Nazi takeover in 1933, and many Nazis themselves, were at pains to stress the peaceful nature of the 'German revolution'. Agreeing with the Nazi Party leader in the Schleswig-Holstein town of Eutin, who boasted of 'how peacefully the revolution has occurred in Germany', they often contrasted the smooth transfer of power in 1933 with the bloodshed and chaos of the revolutionary events in Germany during 1918 and 1919. In 1933 the State did not crumble, the army did not intervene, civil war did not break out. German nationalists could take satisfaction from the apparent orderliness and the absence of large-scale violence which accompanied Hitler's takeover: here, it seemed, was a true 'German' revolution, one during which the trains continued to run on time.

Today this picture of the Nazi seizure of power seems at best rather disingenuous. After all, Nazi activists did not shrink from violence; indeed they gloried in it. Struggle, violence and war were at the centre of Nazi ideology, and for years the Nazi storm troopers, the SA, had been engaged in a campaign of politically motivated street fighting which left hundreds dead and thousands injured during the final years of the Weimar Republic. What is more, Hitler had identified himself publicly with the violent excesses of his followers in a manner hardly typical of leaders of major political parties, when in August 1932 he voiced his 'unbounded loyalty' to a band of Nazis accused of the brutal murder of a Communist sympathiser in the Upper Silesian border village of Potempa. And when, in early 1933, the Nazis finally were able to gain control of interior ministries and police headquarters throughout Germany, storm troopers unleashed a campaign of terror. Thousands of opponents of the Nazis were rounded up and taken away to makeshift concentration camps set up in disused factory premises or barracks, and many met their deaths at the hands of tormentors who, it now appeared, had the power of the German State behind them. Long before Germany was declared officially a one-party State in the summer of 1933, open political activity directed against the Nazis had come to a halt.

The Nazi 'revolution' may not have been as bloody an affair as the Terror following the French Revolution or the Civil War following the Russian, but it was hardly the peaceful, orderly affair that many claimed at the time. Violence was one of the key factors in turning the 'backstairs intrigue' (Alan Bullock's phrase) which brought Hitler to the Reich Chancellory into the first step towards one of the most brutal dictatorships the world has ever seen. While it was the machinations of men of power and influence which put Hitler in the saddle in Berlin, it was the actions of the Nazi storm troopers in cities and towns throughout the country which helped smash opposition to the 'new Germany'.

Immediately upon hearing of the formation of the Hitler government, supporters of political parties took to the streets— the Nazis and their conservative allies to celebrate the 'national uprising' and the Communists to protest against the 'further intensification of the fascist dictatorship'. Fairly typical of what happened were the events in the eastern German city of Breslau (today's Wroclaw) on January 31st. The Communists reacted to the news first, announcing a protest demonstration in the centre of the city at which a general strike was to be proclaimed. But no sooner had the Communists' supporters begun to assemble on the morning of the 31st, than about 500 Nazi storm troopers decided to march through the square where the demonstration was to take place. The police, no friends of the

Communist Party at the best of times and eager to make a positive impression upon their new masters, kept the 500–600 unemployed supporters of the Communists out of the square while the storm troopers paraded around; and when the planned demonstration finally got under way the police quickly intervened to stop it. Police truncheons appeared and the Communists scattered, some running up nearby streets and smashing the windows of the shops selling Nazi uniforms; the police then began shooting, and an unemployed labourer was killed; and afterwards the Breslau Police President (no member of the Nazi Party—he was later to be replaced by the regional SA leader Edmund Heines) used the fiasco as an excuse to ban all Communist rallies as a threat to public order.

Thus, within twenty-four hours of Hitler's appointment, political activity by the German Communist Party was effectively driven underground in the Breslau region. The city's Social Democrats, who had adopted a wait-and-see attitude—after all, the Hitler government was a legal government and the SPD leadership was desperately concerned not to give the authorities an excuse for suppressing their organisations—saw the results of the Communist demonstration as a confirmation of the wisdom of their decision to do nothing. That evening, it was the Nazis' turn. They celebrated their victory with a huge demonstration at which an estimated 50,000 people took part; the centre of Breslau, the largest city in eastern Germany, became a sea of swastika flags and marching columns of brown-shirted storm troopers. Politics in Germany would, they thought, never be the same again.

The events immediately following the formation of the Hitler government are revealing in a number of respects. First, they demonstrate the inability of a political movement (the Communists) whose supporters were largely unemployed to force a show-down with the new government by calling for mass strikes. Second, they show the reluctance of the Social Democrats to commit their forces (which, with the largest

German trade-union federation, workers' sport organisations and a large political defence formation of their own, the *Reichsbanner*, were not inconsiderable) to the struggle. And third, they show that initially it was the police, not the storm troopers, who appear to have taken the initiative in suppressing the Left.

The turn of the storm troopers was to come later. A major step was the formation, in later February, of 'auxilliary police' composed of members of the SA, the SS and the Stahlhelm (a conservative veterans' organisation). This meant that to resist a band of SA men, one of whom wore an armband with the inscription '*Hilfspolizei*' was to confront the power of the State; it lent legality to the terror tactics of the storm troopers. The creation of the 'auxiliary police' and the issuing of orders forbidding police from interfering with Nazi formations were followed by an upsurge of Nazi violence directed against the Left, particularly against Social Democrats and the Social Democratic trade unions. Leading members of the left-wing parties were arrested, as the police and Nazi formations increasingly co-ordinated their activities; attempts by the Social Democrats or Communists to hold election rallies were broken up with growing frequency; the left-wing press—first that of the Communists and then that of the Social Democrats—was suppressed; and by the time of the Reichstag elections on March 5th Nazi violence and police repression had combined effectively to drive the Left from public view.

Nevertheless, although the Nazis had succeeded in paralysing the SPD and driving the Communist Party underground, the main organisational supports of German Social Democracy and the most important source of potential resistance to Nazi dictatorship, the trade unions, remained intact. But once the need to help the Nazi Party with the election campaigns was past, the storm troopers turned their attentions to the root-and-branch destruction of the German trade-union movement. This was not done by a co-ordinated assault throughout the country or by a frontal attack upon the trade-union headquarters in

Berlin. Rather, it was carried out, during March and April, in a piecemeal manner. One day it was the turn of the Breslau trade-union headquarters, taken by the storm troopers after shots were fired when SA men marched in the front of the building; two days later storm troopers hoisted the swastika flag on the trade-union headquarters in Leipzig; a few days later groups of storm troopers laid waste to trade-union offices in Dresden; then it was the turn of trade-unionists of Schneidemühl, then Reutlingen, then Wiesbaden, then Frankfurt, then Hannover. No one could say when or where the next blow might be struck; no one knew at what point they should make their stand.

So the once-impressive institutional supports of German Social Democracy, which had withstood Bismarck's onslaughts fifty years before, were destroyed piecemeal, by instalments. By the time the Nazi government officially dissolved the trade unions in May and allowed their assets to be swallowed up by the newly created 'German Labour Front', the leaders of the once powerful Social Democratic movement were generals without an army.

This campaign against the Left was all the more effective because of its ambiguous nature. Because there was no single, decisive confrontation, and because it was essentially two-pronged—carried out both within and without the existing legal structure—it was much more difficult to resist. In early 1933 the Nazis' opponents faced apparently spontaneous attacks by marauding bands of storm troopers as well as the authority of the police, and the effectiveness of each was enhanced by the other: the storm troopers presented all the more a threat because behind them—somewhere—stood the State, and police repression was all the more effective because it was enhanced by the extra-legal threat of the SA.

This is not to suggest that had the Left united and made a stand the outcome would have been much better. Although Communists and Social Democrats each blame the other (with some degree of justification) for the split within the German Left, the idea that a united Left would have withstood the onslaught of the Nazis and their conservative allies once they controlled the organs of State power—the police and, if need be, the army—is at best a pipe dream. At a time of horrific unemployment the chief weapon of the Left, the General Strike (which had sunk a right-wing Putsch attempt in 1920), was, to say the least, blunted. And to assert that the gulf which separated Socialists and Communists was the making of a few self-seeking politicians is to display a deep misunderstanding of both working-class politics and working-class life in interwar Germany.

For the disagreements on the Left were not merely differences over ideology or attitudes towards the USSR, they also reflected deep social divisions: between the unemployed and those who still hung on to work; between the young and their elders; between those (Social Democrats) who had run the police in Prussia and those (often Communists) against whom the police were deployed, often with bloody results. If the history of the Nazi seizure reveals anything about left-wing politics, it is that there is little the Left can do on its own to stop a powerful right-wing movement which has mass support, allies in powerful places, and control of the repressive apparatus of the State. Seen in this light, it would appear that neither the Communist nor the Social Democratic responses to the wave of Nazi violence in early 1933 held out many prospects for success. The German Left was up a dead end which had been paved for it long before.

If this is true, it puts into question just how important was political violence for putting the Nazis in the saddle. Perhaps the real service of the storm troopers was less to win a decisive battle with the Left than to demonstrate that no real battle still needed to be fought. What the storm troopers revealed in 1933 was that the impressive organisational network of the Social Democrats was little more than a paper tiger, a house of cards

6

that came tumbling down in March and April 1933. This was, to be sure, an important service to the new regime, for Hitler and his allies did not know in advance how easy it would be to dispose of the trade-union movement. The street violence against the Left in 1933 carried very little risk for Germany's new rulers. Because it was a largely spontaneous, apparently uncoordinated assault, had it run up against stiff opposition the new government could have disowned it quickly—as Hitler, Hess and the new Nazi Interior Minister Wilhelm Frick were to do with other unwelcome violent outbursts. But once it was successful then the new regime could take full advantage of it.

The confusion which accompanied the creation of the German Labour Front—its leader, Robert Ley, later confessed to having had little idea in May 1933 what his new organisation was supposed to do—seems to confirm the largely unplanned nature of the assault on the Left. But unplanned though it may have been, it nevertheless had far-reaching repercussions for the social and political history of the Third Reich. Most importantly, it committed the new regime to an uncompromising policy towards trade unions. By April 1933 it was clear that there would be no legal independent labour organisations in the 'new Germany'. Working-class interests and working-class protest would have to be expressed in other ways.

Another important consequence of the terror campaign was that it served to cut the links between the Left and the working class. Within a matter of weeks it became virtually impossible for Social Democrats or Communists to hold rallies, distribute literature, to canvass opinion. With Socialist and Communist party functionaries increasingly likely to be imprisoned, many understandably feared making political contacts. The publicising in the newspapers of the arrests and raids by police and SA served to heighten the fear. As a result, the party leaderships were cut off from the party organisations and the party organisations were cut off from the German people. And the fact that this destruction of the German Left was accomplished in an atmosphere of fear and terror was to colour social and political relations between the German working class and the regime for the life of the Third Reich.

Of course, the Left did not provide the only targets for the violent street politics of the Nazis. Another, obvious target was the Jews. Yet the Nazi violence against German Jews in 1933 was different, both in its timing and its political significance, from the campaign against the Left. For one thing, there was no chance that the Jews would offer physical resistance; largely isolated and defenceless, by 1933 German Jews were objects, not subjects, of German politics. For another, the Jews were largely irrelevant to the campaign for political power of which the struggle against the Left formed a major part. And whereas there is some evidence that the campaigns against the Communists brought the Nazis popular support in 1933, the opposite appears to have been the case with regard to the excesses against the Jews.

For the reasons mentioned above, the assault on Germany's Jews took second place in early 1933 behind the assault on the Left. Indeed, before the elections in March there appears to have been very little violence directed against Jews or Jewish targets. It was not really until mid-March, after Goering (who controlled the Prussian police) announced during a speech in Essen that he rejected the idea that 'the police are a protection squad for Jewish shops', that things changed. This, it appears, was taken as a signal by the Nazis' activist followers, who enforced a growing number of boycotts of Jewish-owned shops, intimidated Jewish individuals and took a number of Jews into custody.

However, although the Nazi leadership had been quite clear in its attitude towards the Jews, its response to this upsurge in anti-Semitic violence was ambivalent. It obviously could not be condemned outright; after all the Nazis' activist supporters were only carrying the anti-Semitic exhortations of the leadership to logical conclusions. Yet there was concern that the SA rank and file should not get out of the control of their leaders and that retail trade, so important to economic recovery, should not be disturbed. Therefore, while Goering appears to have given a blank cheque to the storm troopers, other Nazi leaders, including Hitler, called for discipline and an end to interference in Germany's retail trade. Yet the boycotts did not stop. Faced with a growing boycott movement, evidence that storm troopers were not necessarily heeding the calls for moderation and vociferous protests about the violence from abroad, the Nazi leadership decided to take action: unable to stop the boycotts, the Nazi leadership decided to put itself at their head, and Hitler and Goebbels called for a one-day nationwide boycott of Jewish businesses on Saturday, April 1st Julius Streicher, the notorious anti-Semite and Nazi Party Gauleiter in Nürnberg, was put in charge of the 'Central Committee' which was to co-ordinate the event. This, it was claimed, would be the German people's righteous response to the 'lies' and 'atrocity propaganda' circulating in the foreign press.

Although storm troopers in many towns did not wait for the official signal to begin—there was, if anything, an increase in the number of unofficial boycotts of Jewish businesses in the run-up to April 1st—the day itself passed off fairly peacefully. Throughout the Reich brown-shirted young men took up posts outside Jewish businesses, admonishing people not to go inside, and the 'co-ordinated' German press praised the orderly way in which the boycott had been carried out. Yet the Nazi leadership could hardly claim unqualified success. Support for the boycott was less than total: in many areas Germans demonstratively bought from the black-listed businesses. Indeed, one local Nazi party leader advised subsequently that, 'in the future actions against the Jews must be kept secret': announcing the boycott in advance had only allowed Germans to express their support for its victims by patronising Jewish shops on the preceding Thursday and Friday. If the object of the boycott was to put an end to the unplanned and spontaneous attacks of the previous weeks, however, it appears to have been moderately successful. The boycotts did not stop completely after April 1st, but their number decreased sharply.

The contrast between the campaigns against the Jews and against the Left is revealing of the nature and uses of Nazi violence in early 1933. Like the campaign against the Left, the violence against the Jews appears to have been largely un-planned and uncoordinated (at least until the Nazi leadership intervened in late March); unlike the campaign against the Left, however, the attacks on the Jews involved mostly actions against *economic* targets, aroused widespread misgivings amongst the German public and abroad, and did not offer compensating political dividends since this campaign was essentially irrelevant to the struggle for political power. It is revealing that never again in the history of the Third Reich was there such an attempt to mobilise popular involvement in a nationwide anti-Semitic campaign; never again did the Nazi leaders allow either Julius Streicher or their activist supporters to determine the pace of the assault on the Jews.

Even more problematic for the Nazis were the actions taken during early 1933 against department and chain stores, the 'interferences in the economy' which were condemned by Nazi leaders with increasing frequency in the first half of 1933. For years the Nazis made political capital out of the fear and ant-agonism of small shopkeepers towards their larger competitors, and before 1933 the opening of a new department store branch was invariably the occasion for Nazi protests. Once Hitler was in the Reich Chancellory and the storm troopers felt they could do as they liked, it was not surprising that department and foreign-owned chain stores as well as Jewish shops became targets for boycott actions. Woolworth, Bata (the Czech shoe manufacturer and retailer) and the large department-store chains were favourite targets. But such activities brought strong protests from the firms on the receiving end, as well as concern by the new government about the damage this might be doing to economic recovery; after all, the department stores may have been 'annihilating the *Mittelstand*' but they also were major employers.

It often has been asserted that in the actions of the SA, particularly against institutions such as the large department stores, we can see evidence of the 'socialism' of National Socialism being taken seriously. However, the violent outbursts of the SA involved certain types of capitalist concerns. The targets were almost exclusively retail outlets; industrial plants, corporate offices and commercial banks were largely spared. The Nazi activists had taken their aim not at the capitalist system as a whole but at the most visible capitalist enterprises, ones seen to be inflicting damage directly upon a significant section of the Nazi Party membership and support.

It was these sorts of actions, which were out of step with the needs of the Nazi leadership in Berlin and which provided apparent evidence that the SA was getting out of control, that helped pave the way for the bloody purge of 1934. The SA, which had grown by leaps and bounds during 1933 and had taken into its ranks large numbers of people whose political reliability was (from the Nazis' point of view) highly questionable, was causing increasing difficulties for the regime. Brown-shirted activists persisted in violent activities which were being condemned with growing stridency by the Nazi leadership—in particular by Reich Interior Minister Frick—and the SA was becoming intensely unpopular among the population at large. It is hardly surprising that an organisation of young men who often drank, were rowdy, threatened respectable citizens (and on occasion even the police) with concentration camps, frequently appeared out of the control of its own leaders and numbered millions of members by early 1934, would arouse unease among large sections of the German population. This is, of course, not to assert that the reasons for the purge are to be found in the violent activities mentioned above; the main reasons for the purge lie in the relations of the new government

11

with the armed forces and the unwillingness of SA Chief of Staff Ernst Röhm to give up his idea of the SA becoming a new Nazi people's army. However, the extent of the purge at local level and the tremendous enthusiasm with which it was greeted by most Germans was due in large measure to the continuing, politically counterproductive violence of the brownshirts in late 1933 and early 1934. The SA fell victim to a campaign whereby the Nazi State was constructed so that, as the West German researcher Mathilde Jamin has put it, 'the unpolitical German could regard National Socialist institutions as a constituent part of his bourgeois normality'.

Who, then, was responsible for the wave of violence on which the Nazis rode to power in early 1933, and why did it occur? The answers to these questions are far from clear. To begin with, the SA was an organisation which grew tremendously after Hitler came to power. Even before 1933, when storm troopers were supposed to be members of the Nazi Party—before joining the SA could be regarded as a means to secure employment—membership in the organisation had fluctuated wildly: available statistics point to a membership turnover of perhaps 20–25 per cent in a single month; the SA was an organisation in which someone who had been a member for six months was an experienced veteran. The turnover was all the greater when, after January 1933, the SA was opened officially to people who were not party members, and membership rose from roughly half a million at the time of Hitler's appointment as Reich Chancellor to about three million a year later.

Nevertheless, despite the difficulties a few general comments can be made: Nazi activists were young—the vast majority of SA men, over 80 per cent, were under thirty; a large proportion were workers (not surprising considering the age structure of the SA), even if, relative to the population as a whole, workers were not really over-represented; many were unemployed, particularly those who made their homes in 'SA barracks' and formed the activist backbone of the organisation; and all, obviously, were male.

This last point, while perhaps obvious, is important. Nazi activism was a predominantly male preserve; Nazi violence a product of a political culture which praised 'male' virtues of toughness and standing one's ground. It was a great achievement of the Nazi movement that it so successfully channelled the violent behaviour of young men into domestic politics. Indeed, it is possible to see the violence of the Nazis (and of their opponents) as the arrival in the political arena of the sorts of gang violence and fighting which are quite common in modern industrial societies—something which Eve Rosenhaft has shown so brilliantly in her recent work on Communist street fighters during the final Weimar years. The violent behaviour of the young man out to prove his virility, clothed in and justified by the language of radical nationalism and anti-Marxism, proved an extremely powerful political weapon. Thus, far from being (as Peter Merkl has suggested in a recent article) the product of a 'deviant' culture or the expression of personal frustrations of disturbed 'individuals of violent propensity', the Nazis' achievement in attracting and mobilising hundreds of thousands of young men to their cause was due to their success in building upon mainstream social values.

Yet while Nazi activism may have been an expression of an unexceptionally violent culture, the behaviour of the storm troopers was exceptional. Not every advanced industrial society has had to cope with hundreds of thousands of young men organised in uniformed formations battling it out in the streets; not every advanced industrial society has settled political differences with the concentration camp. It was the specific social and economic context of Germany during the early 1930s which allowed the National Socialist movement to grow and to exploit the energies of hundreds of thousands of people. Among the most important factors which made this possible was mass unemployment. While the great mass of the unemployed no doubt reacted to their fate with resignation, frustration and apathy—which has been described and analysed so memorably in the justly famous study of *The Unemployed of Marienthal*—a large number of young men did not. It is clear that the sort of politics pursued by Nazi activists, a politics which required a tremendous amount of time and energy, was hardly compatible with full-time employment. Only a minority of Nazi supporters may have conformed to the picture of the dedicated, 'fanatic' Nazi activist, the full-time 'political soldier' who often was housed in SA barracks and fed in SA soup kitchens, and who participated in rally after rally, march after march. But they were enough. The combination of mass unemployment, the breakdown of traditional political allegiances which characterised Weimar politics, and a culture which embraced violent aggressive values lifted the Nazi movement from relative obscurity to become the most successful practitioner of violent street politics that Germany had ever seen.

That said, it is important not to exaggerate the violent nature of Nazi politics and the importance of political violence in the Nazi capture of power. In the first place, as noted above, Hitler was not given the keys to the Reich Chancellory by violent storm troopers but by the 'old guard', keen to make a deal ensuring that Germany did not return to genuine democracy after the dismantling of the Weimar Constitution from 1930 onwards. Secondly, Nazi violence had its limits. Hitler had seen the folly in 1923 of openly courting confrontation with the forces of law and order, when his coup attempt died an ignominious death at the hands of the army in Munich; for sound tactical reasons the Nazi Party of the early 1930s, the mass movement, was committed to achieving power by legal means. And Nazi activists generally appreciated this. It is common for historians to stress how widespread was Nazi violence, but some thought also should be given to its limits. Nazi activists may have been 'fanatics', but they were not such fanatics as to stage frontal assaults on the State. Attacks by the SA on police stations or army barracks—that is upon targets where real resistance could be expected and whereby real issues of political power were at stake—were conspicuous by their absence. The storm troopers generally steered well clear of out-and-out terrorism, and the one time when this did erupt—in August 1932—it was dealt with effectively by the police and soon repudiated by the Nazi leadership. A comparison with the events which accompanied the demise of parliamentary government in Turkey a few years ago—when thousands were killed in an orgy of political violence—or the campaigns of the IRA in Northern Ireland over the past fifteen years suggests how limited was the violence in which the Nazis were engaged. The Nazi movement did not so much engage in the politics of terrorism as the politics of hooliganism.

Yet even this was paradoxical. Nazism may have mobilised violence and hooliganism, but it also did so in the defence of the social order. It simultaneously promised radical change and upholding of traditional values. It appealed to both roughness and respectability. The SA proved a draw both because it appealed to young men keen to prove their manliness and because it was a hierarchical organisation which put young men into uniforms and structured their lives. As the destroyer of Marxism it could pose as the defender of order; indeed, this pose of violence in the defence of order is one of the central paradoxes which explains the success of the Nazi movement both in attracting support and in being able to consolidate the dictatorship so quickly in 1933. As such, the politics of violence played a key role in the rise of the Nazi movement and in the capture of power in 1933, but as the purge of 1934 indicates, its usefulness to Germany's new masters was limited. Once the grip of the Nazi dictatorship had been established, it was the turn of the SS.

VILLAGE LIFE IN NAZI GERMANY

Gerhard Wilke

THE village of Körle in northern Hesse is situated in hilly countryside along the Fulda River, about 20 kilometres south of the town of Kassel (not far from today's East–West German border). Built on the main historical trade route of the region—the Nürnberger Landstrasse—the village had early links with the regional market centres of Melsungen, Kassel, Rotenburg and Hersfeld; and communications were greatly improved by the building of a railway through the village in 1848 and the opening of a local station in 1892. Largely because the railway made it possible for people to live in Körle and work in Kassel, the village did not suffer the decline which affected many other rural communities as people left for the city: in 1864 Körle had 595 inhabitants; by 1895 its population stood at 619; and by 1939 it had risen to 1,039, all Protestant.

Although industrialisation had affected life in Körle in the nineteenth century, the Weimar years still are regarded as a period of major economic and social, as well as political, upheaval. Between 1918 and 1933 the 'traditional' village society began to disintegrate and change. The village population continued to grow; it became harder for households to make a living from agriculture; and the need for urban employment increased. However, as soon as more villagers were sucked into the world of urban employment, they were confronted by the catastrophic unemployment of the final Weimar years and were thrown back onto village society and their households for support. At the same time, the Weimar Republic brought a democratisation to local political and cultural institutions and, by implication, began to threaten the previously unchallenged power of traditional village élites. One might have expected such developments to lead to open conflict in the village. This

17

did not happen, however. Instead, scapegoats from beyond village society became the main targets for blame: Jews, capitalists, Communists, the victorious Allies.

During the 1920s most village households were involved in a 'double economy' and derived their income from both agricultural and industrial work. The majority remained within the village economy with only one or two members of each household holding down an industrial or office job. The possession of land, a house, and the ability to work on the land remained central to regulating everyday life in the village and formed the basis for status and prestige.

Villagers who owned 'a lot of land' (10–30 hectares) were known as 'horse farmers'; they produced food for the market, employed both full-time and casual labour on their farms and constituted the ruling village élite. The owners of 'less but still quite a lot of land' (1–9 hectares) were classified as 'cow farmers' because they used cows rather than horses as draft animals. These households could not live solely off the land. Finally, those villagers who owned a 'small strip of land' (0.1–1.0 hectares) or rented an allotment and who possessed no draft animals for cultivation were called 'goat farmers'. These households relied on industrial wages as their main source of income but tried to be self-sufficient in food. To this end they hired out their labour to the horse farmers on a casual basis and in return their land was ploughed. The 'worker-peasants' regarded their home-grown food as indispensible to their household economy and were determined to defend themselves against the greater poverty and insecurity they associated with the life-style of their urban working-class colleagues—a mentality which was reinforced by the catastrophic unemployment of the late 1920s and early 1930s.

During the Weimar period a class-consciousness based on industrial and State employment started to affect the public life of the village. Local branches of the SPD (Social Democrats) and the KPD (Communists) were formed and the existing recreational clubs in the village split into socialist and nationalist ones. The split in the clubs reflected the local hierarchy: the new clubs and the SPD and KPD branches represented the beginnings of a working-class counter-culture to the conservative and nationalist counterparts, which were the political power base of the horse farmers and their allies within the village. And in creating this 'counter-culture' the SPD and KPD activists mobilised enough support in the village during the Weimar years to prevent the Nazis from ever gaining an absolute majority in a free local election.

The oppositional effect of the new working-class culture should not be overestimated, however. Both the Social Democratic and Communist organisations in the village reproduced 'traditional' ideology. All village clubs, irrespective of political affiliation, excluded women from positions of responsibility, and all shared a concern for representing the honour of the village *vis-à-vis* the outside world and thereby reproduced the myth of the community spirit (*'Dorfgemeinschaft'*). Sports competitions and public festivals, organised by the village clubs, became a 'safe' way of expressing and controlling the threat posed by the new class politics. This enabled villagers to maintain neighbourly relations, despite deepening social and political differences. It also paved the way for continued co-operation with the existing village élites. The horse farmers were able to preserve their domination of the village economy and political power structure by providing casual employment for the worker-peasants and by exploiting the cow farmers' fear of social decline. This system of social domination was based upon the traditional paternalistic authority of the older generation of horse farmers. The problem, however, was that their children could no longer see themselves as automatic heirs to this position in the village hierarchy, and they became attracted to Nazism.

The local branch of the Nazi party in Körle was formed in 1928 by the sons of the horse and cow farmers. They were disillusioned with their fathers' yearning for a return of the Monarchy, feared the threat posed by the Left, and wanted radical solutions to three 'existential' and 'ideological' problems: the survival of their generation as independent farmers, the preservation of their political dominance, and the suppression of their 'enemies' (the Jews and the working class).

Though Nazi activists in the village regularly participated in regionally organised Nazi Party rallies, it took them until 1932 to put up candidates in local parish elections. Then they gained two seats on the council, and with the Communists remained one of the smallest parties. The picture was different in the national and regional elections after 1929, where the Nazis, Social Democrats and Communists each attracted more votes than the Nationalists, who continued to dominate local politics until they were forcibly replaced by the Nazis in the spring of 1933.

The first and most significant steps in the consolidation of Nazi power within the village in 1933 were the replacement of the Nationalist mayor, the banning of Social Democratic and Communist Parties and the abolition of recreational clubs associated with the Left. This *Gleichschaltung* (ideological coordination) of social and political life was carried out without significant resistance. In anticipation of possible tensions, the Nazi Party consciously chose to bring in storm troopers from neighbouring villages to seize the assets of the working-class organisations, and villagers criticised the personal behaviour of the outsiders rather than the political system and its local representatives.

The lack of a coherent critique of the regime must not, however, be interpreted as total compliance. Many villagers were enraged by the events they witnessed. Some resisted the Nazi attack on the working-class organisations; others voted with their feet and avoided public parades. When the storm troopers came to confiscate the bicycles of the Communist cycling club, the publican in whose inn the club met refused to hand them over, claiming that he had part-ownership; after the Second World War he handed the bikes back to their rightful owners. When the Nazis held their first May Day parade, they found themselves passing the flag of the Weimar Republic hoisted by a local woman.

Nevertheless, open acts of defiance were rare and, in general, the regime did win the approval of most villagers during its early years in power. The Nazis were successful in convincing people that they could provide increased employment and reduce poverty. They gained popularity through the introduction of the *Arbeitsdienst* (Labour Service), the establishment of separate organisations for women and youngsters, the 'Strength-through-Joy' programme of cheap package holidays and the ruthless persecution of deviants and minorities. Though most of the working-class activists and many of the older generation remained opposed to the regime and demonstrated their disapproval by staying away from public displays of Nazi power, many got caught up in the patriotic euphoria of the mid-1930s.

Nazi politics led to important changes in the village households as regards authority structures and the position of women and children. The village law, 'your own household above all else in the world', was undermined as the Nazi takeover altered existing social relationships. Generally, the older generation remained sceptical of the Nazis, while the younger generation became active in the movement. This resulted in conflict between the generations: sons, and later daughters, who were prominent within the various Nazi organisations carried their newly found confidence and fervour into their own homes and challenged their parents. Villagers still describe this period as one which witnessed 'war in every household', as loyalty and obligations to Nazi Party and State organisations conflicted with the wishes of the older generation.

During the Third Reich the household lost its dominant role in the rearing and training of children. The school became an instrument for the dissemination of racial propaganda, helped to win young minds for the system and made them receptive to militaristic ideas and practices. The Hitler Youth conveyed ideals that extended beyond the terms of reference of the traditional village upbringing. The time children previously would have spent working on the land was taken up with keep-fit, survival and other para-military exercises—which the youngsters thought was 'a lot of fun'. Young men and women were conscripted into military or labour services, and this affected the household's ability to cope at peak periods of the agricultural cycle and caused resentment against both the younger generation and the political system.

However, generational conflict did not produce open resistance because people were caught in an ideological trap. The Nazi State justified the introduction of these changes in the same terms in which a head of household would have rationalised using everyone's labour to feed the household and uphold its good name. In both cases the subjection to authoritarian rule and the use of cheap labour were justified by the claim that 'everyone's welfare was at stake'; concern with the individual's needs was regarded as synonymous with irresponsibility.

The Nazi regime also brought tremendous changes to the lives of women in the village. The Nazis introduced village women to public life; they founded separate women's organisations; and they introduced a form of national service for girls. The National Socialist Organisation of Women (*Frauenschaft*), the League of German Girls (BDM) and the Labour Service had not only an ideological retraining function. They also allowed women to travel beyond the narrow confines of the village, brought them in contact with women from other regions and made them cross social class-boundaries. Furthermore, military and labour service helped to relax the principally endogamous marriage patterns which had prevailed in the village. In short, Nazism brought a certain 'liberation' from the traditional confines of village life.

However, in many other spheres the changes brought about by Nazism were far from liberating. In fact, demands on women increased during the Third Reich. As the regime moved towards war, women were expected increasingly to combine the roles of mother, housewife, Party member and industrial worker. The reintroduction of conscription and later on war service deprived households of their male agricultural labour. Women, children and the old had to fill the gap. During the war, women took over the management of most farms (with the exception of those of the horse farmers, who were freed from military service in order to produce food). Before 1934 none of the girls who left school had taken an apprenticeship or received vocational training; after 1935 this happened increasingly. Girls took up urban employment and brought home additional wages. However, the war brought changes here as well. On the one hand, the extra cash brought to the household kitty by women employed in the city was rendered insignificant when the economy came to be dominated by barter and black-market rules after 1943. On the other hand, women factory workers were increasingly subjected to military discipline as they worked side by side with prisoners-of-war and were supervised by armed guards. For the first time village women experienced the full force of undisguised State power.

Before the war, the villages always had resisted the influx of large numbers of outsiders, which they feared would threaten the integrity and identity of their community. The war, and the administrative measures of the Nazi State, changed this and forced them to accept strangers. From 1939 onwards, each household in the village had to accommodate evacuees (from bomb-threatened cities) and refugees, who were allocated by a commission appointed by the Nazi mayor. This commission inspected each house and decided how much space had to be made available. The removal of authority over one's own property was met not with enthusiastic patriotism, but with resignation and silent anger. The intrusion into the house, the most important symbol of a household's independence and self-respect, together with the reports being received from surviving relatives at the front and the efforts of the State to regulate food production, convinced most villagers that the Third Reich had outlived its usefulness. From 1944 onwards some people openly began to defy the officials of the regime by not declaring food which they had produced. In a few cases villagers even hid soldiers on the run. However, Nazi power did not crumble completely in the village; as late as March 1945 the local school teacher intervened to ensure the arrest of some army deserters.

By May 1945 the social and political composition of the village had changed for good. The old order had been broken up by the administrative and military intrusions of the Nazi organisations. The structure of Körle's population also had significantly altered. Virtually every household had suffered a loss at the front, most of the dead were young men, and the proportion of older people and women in the population thus had increased. The massive influx of evacuees and refugees, as a consequence of the bombings and the forceful evacuation of Germans from eastern Germany, meant that the number of people living in Körle had doubled, although the available housing had not. The drift away from agricultural to industrial occupations, especially for women, was accelerated by the imposition of the war economy and the large number of war widows. The political landscape of the village was turned upside down as the Allies eventually restored democratic institutions and as the political stranglehold of the traditional élites (the horse farmers who were discredited by their association with Nazi organisations and their shameless profiteering on the wartime black market) was finally broken. Far from ensuring that a German rural way of life based on '*Blut und Boden*' (blood and soil) would endure, the Nazis had unleashed forces which effectively destroyed the 'traditional' structure of village life.

YOUTH IN THE THIRD REICH

Detlev Peukert

DURING the twelve years of the Nazi state three separate age groups passed through adolescence, that is the years between the fourteenth and eighteenth birthdays. Each group had its own distinctive experiences.

Those whose adolescence fell in the years 1933–6 had already had important, formative experiences before the Nazi seizure of power. They were in the front line for incorporation into the Hitler Youth and the so-called *Volksgemeinschaft* (racial community) of the Third Reich. They had also experienced the economic crisis of the early 1930s and were therefore quite receptive to the benefits offered by the rearmament programme (particularly after 1935–6), as well as to the ideas of *Führerstaat* (leadership state), with its promise of an end to 'party squabbles', and of the 'restoration of national greatness'.

The young people of the period 1936–9 had no such memories. They had gone through schools that bore the stamp of National Socialism. For many, adolescence shaped by the Hitler Youth was something taken for granted and to which there was no alternative. Against group comradeship and leisure activities, occasional irritations in the form of brutality and intolerance, drill and demagogy, were often insignificant. And what is more, the Hitler Youth—as a rival to the traditional authorities of home and school—could to some extent serve as a 'counter-authoritarian' sanctuary. Involvement in its activities thus offered simultaneously the promise of making a name for oneself but also growing pressure towards uniformity. This latter feature grew stronger as the Hitler Youth became more bureaucratic, as its leadership corps grew older, and as the use of coercion to draw remaining young people into the organisation increased.

The age group whose adolescence occurred during the war years 1939–45 experienced particularly the empty aspects of daily life in the Hitler Youth, characterised by coercion and drill. Quite a few youth leaders were conscripted into the army, and from 1942–3 onwards many club buildings and sports fields were destroyed by the bombings. With this 'war generation' the grip of National Socialist institutions was simultaneously at its most far-reaching and increasingly repellent.

National Socialist youth policy aimed to secure the younger generation's total loyalty to the regime and their willingness to fight in the war that lay ahead. All competitors had to be eliminated and Nazi forms of organisation and militaristic education developed. These tasks were to be achieved with the distinctively Nazi combination of compulsion and prohibitions on the one hand and incentives and enticements on the other.

In practice, contradictions arose between these objectives of youth policy, and particularly between the different methods of realising them: contradictions which fragmented and obstructed what appeared at first sight to be a uniform programme of totalitarian assimilation. For example, military conscription robbed the Hitler Youth of many badly needed older youth leaders. Competition between the rival authorities of school and the Hitler Youth gave rise to areas of conflict in which young people could play the one off against the other. And, not least, the ideological content of National Socialism remained much too vague. Fragmentary notions of racial and national arrogance were mixed up with traditional pedagogic humanism: the model of the front-line soldier mixed up with the idea that there was an especially profound and valuable 'German' culture; backward-looking agrarian Romanticism mixed up with enthusiasm for modern technology.

The life stories of young people under the swastika often contain the most contradictory impressions. If there was any common denominator, it was an education in the reckless, ruthless pursuit of genuine or inculcated interests. The following extract hints at how this came about:

No one in our class ever read *Mein Kampf*. I myself only took quotations from the book. On the whole we didn't know much about Nazi ideology. Even anti-Semitism was brought in rather marginally at school—for example via Richard Wagner's essay 'The Jews in Music' —and outside school the display copies of *Der Stürmer* made the idea questionable, if anything. . . . Nevertheless, we were politically programmed: to obey orders, to cultivate the soldierly 'virtue' of standing to attention and saying 'Yes, Sir', and to stop thinking when the magic word 'Fatherland' was uttered and Germany's honour and greatness were mentioned.

War seemed 'normal'; violence seemed 'legitimate'. Hitler's foreign policy achievements between 1936 and 1939 had accustomed the Germans to regard the combination of violent posturing, assertion of their 'legal right' to wipe out the 'shame of Versailles', and risk-taking as a recipe for success.

The main arm of National Socialist youth policy was the Hitler Youth. By the end of 1933 all youth organisations, apart from the Catholic ones (which for the time being remained protected owing to the Nazi government's Concordat with the Vatican), had been either banned (like the socialist youth movement) or 'co-ordinated' more or less voluntarily and integrated into the Hitler Youth (like the non-political *bündisch* youth movement and, in late 1933/early 1934, the Protestant organisations).

By the end of 1933, therefore, the Hitler Youth already contained 47 per cent of boys aged between ten and fourteen (in the *Deutsches Jungvolk*) and 38 per cent of boys between fourteen and eighteen (in the Hitler Youth proper). However, only 15 per cent of girls between ten and fourteen were organised (in the *Jungmädelbund* and only 8 per cent of those between fifteen and twenty-one (in the *Bund Deutscher Mädel*). The Hitler Youth Law of December 1st, 1936, called for the incorporation of all German youth, and this was backed up with growing pressure on those remaining outside to enrol 'voluntarily'—until two executive orders ancillary to the Hitler Youth Law, issued on March 25th, 1939, made 'youth service' compulsory.

In the years immediately following 1933, many did not regard membership in the Hitler Youth as compulsory. The Hitler Youth built upon many practices of the youth organisations of the Weimar period, offered a wide range of leisure activities, and, at the lower levels (which in the everyday running of things were the most important), was led not infrequently by people who had had previous experience in other youth organisations. In addition, the Hitler Youth uniform often provided the chance to engage, sometimes quite aggressively, in conflict with traditional figures of authority: the teacher, the father, the foreman, the local clergyman.

For many young people in the provinces, where the youth movement was not widespread before 1933, the arrival of the Hitler Youth often meant the first access to the leisure activities in a youth organisation, the impetus to build a youth club or sports field, or the opportunity to go on weekend or holiday trips away from one's narrow home environment.

The emancipatory openings for girls were even greater. In the *Bund Deutscher Mädel* girls could escape from the female role-model centred around family and children—a role-model which, for that matter, was also propagated by the National Socialists. They could pursue activities which were otherwise reserved for boys; and if they worked as functionaries for the *Bund Deutscher Mädel* they might even approach the classic 'masculine' type of the political organiser who was never at home. Such opportunities remained limited, however, and were withdrawn increasingly owing to the Nazis' general discrimination against women. Yet these groups undoubtedly proved, in many practical day-to-day respects, to be a modernising force.

With the consolidation of the Hitler Youth as a large-scale

bureaucratic organisation, and with the gradual ageing of its leadership cadres in the course of the 1930s, the movements' attraction to the young people began to decline. Political campaigns within the Hitler Youth against those who had been leaders in the Weimar youth movement and against styles and behaviour allegedly associated with that organisation led to the disciplining and purging of units. The campaign to bring everyone into the Hitler Youth ranks brought in those who previously had proclaimed their antipathy simply by their absence. Disciplinary and surveillance measures to enforce 'youth service' made even harmless everyday pleasures such as meetings of friends and cliques criminal offences. Above all, the claim of legal power by Hitler Youth patrols, whose members were scarcely older than the young people they were keeping track of, provoked general indignation. And in addition, even before the outbreak of war, the Hitler Youth concentrated increasingly on premilitary drill.

The belief that the Hitler Youth successfully mobilised young people is only half the story. The more the Hitler Youth arrogated state powers to itself and the more completely it drew young people into its organisation, the more obvious became the examples of deviant behaviour among adolescents. By the end of the 1930s thousands of young people were turning away from the leisure activities of the Hitler Youth and finding their own unregimented style in independent gangs. Indeed, they defended their independence all the more insistently as Hitler Youth patrols and the Gestapo increased their pressure. In 1942 the Reich Youth Leadership had to admit:

The formation of cliques, i.e. groupings of young people outside the Hitler Youth, has been on the increase before and, particularly, during the war to such a degree that one must speak of a serious risk of the political, moral and criminal subversion of youth.

The leadership could not now make the excuse that the people involved had been conditioned by the Weimar 'system': by

'Marxism', 'clericalism' or the old youth movements. The adolescents who made up this opposition in the late 1930s and early 1940s were the very generation on whom Adolf Hitler's system had operated unhindered.

Amidst the wealth of evidence of unaccommodating behaviour, two groups stand out particularly clearly, groups which shared a rejection of the Hitler Youth but which differed in their styles, backgrounds and actions: the 'Edelweiss Pirates' (*Edelweisspiraten*) and the 'Swing Youth' (*Swing-Jugend*).

The first Edelweiss Pirates appeared at the end of the 1930s in western Germany. The names of the individual groups, their badges (metal edelweiss flowers worn on the collar, the skull and crossbones, pins with coloured heads), their dress (usually a checked shirt, dark short trousers, white socks) and their activities all varied, but were based upon a single underlying model. 'Roving Dudes' from Essen, 'Kittelbach Pirates' from Oberhausen or Düsseldorf (named after a stream in the north of Düsseldorf) and 'Navajos' from Cologne all regarded themselves as 'Edelweiss Pirate' groups. This agreement took on real meaning during weekend trips into the surrounding countryside, where groups from the whole region met up, pitched tents, sang, talked, and together 'bashed' Hitler Youth patrols doing their rounds.

The opposition—the Hitler Youth, Gestapo and the law—also soon categorised the groups under a single heading, having first wavered in case the 'youth movement' (*bündisch*) label would save them the bother of having to analyse new, spontaneous forms of oppositional activity and construct corresponding new sets of prohibitions. It soon became clear, however, that although it was possible to spot precursor groups and so-called 'wild' *bündisch* organisations in the early 1930s, there was no continuity of personnel (the 'delinquents' of 1935–7 long since had been conscripted to the front) and there was no direct ideological line of descent.

The Edelweiss Pirate groups arose spontaneously, as young

people aged between fourteen and eighteen got together to make the most of their free time away from the control of the Hitler Youth. The age composition of the group, with a clustering around it of younger children and older war-wounded men and women in reserved occupations, was not fortuitous: boys of seventeen and eighteen were conscripted into the National Labour Service and then into the Wehrmacht, while at fourteen boys reached the school-leaving age and could thus escape from the immediate, day-to-day sphere of Hitler Youth control. They were taking their first steps into work—as apprentices or, thanks to the shortage of manpower caused by the war, increasingly as relatively well-paid unskilled workers. To an increased sense of self-esteem and independence the continuing obligation of Hitler Youth service up to the age of eighteen could contribute very little. The war reduced the Hitler Youth's leisure attractions: instead there was repeated paramilitary drill with pointless exercises in obedience, which were all the more irksome for being supervised by Hitler Youth leaders scarcely any older than the rank and file, yet who often stood out by the virtue of their grammar or secondary-school background. 'It's the Hitler Youth's own fault', one Edelweiss Pirate from Düsseldorf said, explaining his group's slogan 'Eternal war on the Hitler Youth': 'every order I was given contained a threat.'

The self-confidence of the Edelweiss Pirates and their image among their peers were unmistakable, as an Oberhausen mining instructor found in the case of his trainees in 1941:

Every child knows who the KP [common abbreviation for Kittelbach Pirates] are. They are everywhere; there are more of them than there are Hitler Youth. And they all know each other, they stick close together . . . They beat up the patrols, because there are so many of them. They don't agree with anything. They don't go to work either, they're always down by the canal, at the lock.

The overriding factor common to these groups was the territorial principle: they belonged together because they lived or worked together; and a gang usually consisted of about a dozen boys and a few girls. The fact that girls were involved at all distinguished these oppositional groups from the strictly segregated *Bund Deutscher Mädel* and Hitler Youth. The presence of girls at the evening get-togethers and on the weekend trips into the countryside gave the adolescents a relatively unrestricted opportunity to have sexual experiences. In this respect they were much less prudish than their parents' generation, particularly the representatives of Nazi organisations with their almost obsessive fixation on the repression of sexuality. Nevertheless, sexual life in these groups was no doubt much less orgiastic than contemporary authors of official reports believed, or wanted others to believe, when they sought to construct a trinity of delinquency out of (sexual and criminal) degeneracy, (anti-organisational and anti-authoritarian) rebellion, and (political) opposition.

The high point of the pirates' free time was the weekend, when the young people could go off on hikes. Armed with rucksacks, sheath knives and bread-and-butter rations, sleeping in tents or barns, they spent a carefree time with like-minded young people from other towns—although always on the watch for Hitler Youth patrols, whom they, prudently calculating their own strength, either sought to avoid or taunted and fell upon with relish.

An important reason for this need to get as much space as possible as often as possible between themselves and their everyday conditions was the wish to avoid the 'educative' incursions of adults and the daily experiences of denunciations, spying, orders and punishments by National Socialist institutions that were directly bound up with these incursions. The youth movement's old reason for hiking—to withdraw from the pressures of the adult world—was intensified and given a political dimension in the Third Reich.

It is an astonishing fact that quite a few of these adolescents took long journeys during their holidays, as far as the Black

Forest and the Tirol, to Munich, Vienna and Berlin—and this during wartime, despite bans on travel, restrictions on freedom of movement caused by the system of food ration-cards, and police checks. The youths made ends meet with casual work, hitched lifts, joined up with other hitch-hikers, and in the process demonstrated the existence and vitality of informal structures of support and communication even in the bureaucratised war economy of the Third Reich.

If the long holiday journeys and shorter weekend trips opened up realms of experience that were normally out of the reach of working-class children (especially during the war), the daily meetings after work made possible the development of distinctive identities that marked off the working-class youth subcultures of the Edelweiss Pirates from the dominant, official culture of the Hitler Youth. At these evening gatherings people chatted, told stories, played the guitar and sang songs—especially hiking songs or popular hits about foreign lands, adventure, tough men, beautiful girls. No cliché from the world of commercial entertainment was left unused. Nevertheless, the Edelweiss Pirates appropriated these banal stereotypes for their own ends. For one thing, they were not singing the Hitler Youth songs prescribed as 'suitable for young people' or the fighting songs of the chauvinistic German military tradition; they sang adult hit songs, which dealt with adventure not allowed to the young, with eating, drinking and love. The Edelweiss Pirates developed a remarkable knack for rewriting lyrics—inserting new phrases, lines or whole verses which catapulted their own lives into this dream world.

The Edelweiss Pirates turned the traditional songs of the hiking and youth movements to similar use. They adapted or reworded these songs and used them as signals of protest, either because the songs themselves were disapproved of or even banned by the Hitler Youth or because the names of supposed foes in the original texts were replaced with those of the Nazis, Gestapo or Hitler Youth.

The war years brought an increasing number of clashes between the Edelweiss Pirates and the Hitler Youth. On July 17th, 1943, the Düsseldorf-Grafenberg branch of the Nazi Party reported to the Gestapo:

Re: 'Edelweiss Pirates'. The said youths are throwing their weight around again. I have been told that gatherings of young people have become-more conspicuous than ever [in a local park], especially since the last air raid on Düsseldorf. These adolescents, aged between 12 and 17, hang around into the late evening with musical instruments and young females. Since this riff-raff is in large part outside the Hitler Youth and adopts a hostile attitude towards the organisation, they represent a danger to other young people. It has recently been established that members of the armed forces too are to be found among these young people and they, owing to their membership in the Wehrmacht, exhibit particularly arrogant behaviour. There is a suspicion that it is these youths who have covered the walls of the pedestrian subway on the Altenbergstrasse with the slogans 'Down with Hitler', 'The OKW [*Oberkommando der Wehrmacht*, Military High Command] is lying', 'Medals for Murder', 'Down with Nazi Brutality' etc. However often these inscriptions are removed, within a few days new ones reappear on the walls.

The conflict grew; on the one side was a power apparatus whose drive for perfection led to ever more irrational measures of coercion and surveillance; on the other, gangs of young people who had nothing in their favour apart from their large number and their ability to retreat into the hiding-place of everyday normality.

The Gestapo and Hitler Youth brought to bear an armoury of repressive weapons that ranged from individual warnings, raids and temporary arrest (often followed by release with the public branding of a shaven head) to weekend detention, corrective education, referral to a labour camp, youth concentration camp or criminal trial. Thousands were caught in the net; in a single day, on December 7th, 1942, the Düsseldorf Gestapo broke up the following groups: 28 groups containing

739 adolescents in Düsseldorf, Duisburg, Essen and Wuppertal, including the Cologne Edelweiss Pirates whose so-called ringleaders were publicly hanged in Cologne-Ehrenfeld in November 1944. Indeed, as the curtain was coming down on the Third Reich, the 'Reichsführer SS' and head of the German police (Himmler) issued a decree on October 25th, 1944, on the 'combating of youth gangs', the last in the long series of bans and prosecutions in the attempt to defeat the protest movements.

As long as the Nazis needed armament workers and future soldiers, they could not exterminate German youth as they exterminated the Poles and the Jews; they were forced to use more sophisticated treatment—for their ideological concept of the 'healthy stock of German youth'. But a subculture without organised structures only rarely throws up 'ringleaders' who can easily be singled out. An alternative way of organising free time, which many observe and with which very many more of the same age sympathise, cannot be penalised in blanket fashion. A sceptical attitude towards work, authority, order and morality can be dealt with punitively in individual cases, but not when a considerable portion of the younger generation begins to subscribe to it.

Therefore the institutions of the Nazi State reacted to the Edelweiss Pirate movement with manifest uncertainty. Some State functionaries regarded the offences as silly childish pranks, a result of the degeneration of youth caused by the war and the waning appeal of the Hitler Youth, deprived of its leaders by military conscription. Others smelled large-scale conspiracy and looked for secret organisations, instigators behind the scenes—in other words, projected their own familiar schemata on to a movement they did not understand. But the Edelweiss Pirates were neither simply 'deprived children' nor unimpeachable political resistance fighters. They displayed behaviour that deviated from the desirable social norm with a political rejection of National Socialism, and its maintenance of an authoritarian, hierarchical and militaristic way of life.

All Edelweiss Pirates rejected the Nazis; indeed, this rejection and the elements of an alternative life-style defined them. Few, however, had a definite political point of view, something one can hardly expect in the case of fourteen to eighteen-year-olds. They seem, rather, to have set their own experiences as a group against the specific and abstract demands which National Socialism made on them. None of the Edelweiss Pirates was content with mere passive rejection of Nazism; they wanted to do something against the Hitler Youth, but only a few went beyond everyday acts of petty provocation. These few, however, stuck Allied propaganda leaflets they found in the woods into people's letter boxes, or joined organised resistance groups. In Düsseldorf in 1942 Communists, including the Communist Party leader Wilhelm Knöchjel, made contact with Edelweiss Pirates such as Werner Heyden, received reports on popular opinion from him and gave him stickers and leaflets to distribute. In Cologne-Ehrenfeld in 1944 Edelweiss Pirates joined an underground group which in the maze of bombed streets and houses offered shelter to German army deserters, prisoners of war, forced labourers and prisoners from concentration camps. They got supplies by making armed raids on military depôts, assaulted Nazis and took part in partisan-type attacks—one of which indeed claimed the chief of the Cologne Gestapo in the autumn of 1944.

Thus, members of the Edelweiss Pirate movement spanned the whole range of nonconformist behaviour, from conscious non-participation to open protest and political resistance. The common denominator in all these activities was the creation of a divergent subculture among sections of working-class youth. This derived its political pungency from two sources: in the first place, the rigid power claims of National Socialism could tolerate no deviant behaviour; and secondly, the conflict could also be seen crudely in terms of class conflict between the working-class Pirates and the bourgeois National Socialists. The Edelweiss Pirates rebelled against the Nazi authorities and regimented leisure; their songs, their style of protest, their demeanour indicated that they had seen through the phraseology of the *Volksgemeinschaft.*

A quite different form of popular culture developed among young people from the upper middle class: the 'Swing' movement. Its adherents took every opportunity to avoid *völkische* music and the 'moon-in-June' triviality of German hit tunes in order to listen to jazz and swing numbers, either on records or with live bands. Initially some of these events were allowed to take place in public; then, when Hitler Youth officials took offence at them, they were banned. In one internal Hitler Youth report about a swing festival in Hamburg in February 1940, which was attended by 500–600 adolescents, one can hear all the leitmotifs that pervade the lamentations of authorities faced by the jazz and rock cultures of the twentieth century:

The dance music was all English and American. Only swing dancing and jitterbugging took place. At the entrance to the hall stood a notice on which the words 'Swing prohibited' had been altered to 'Swing requested'. Without exception the participants accompanied the dances and songs by singing the English lyrics. Indeed, throughout the evening they attempted to speak only English; and some tables even French.

The dancers made an appalling sight. None of the couples danced normally; there was only swing of the worst sort. Sometimes two boys danced with one girl; sometimes several couples formed a circle, linking arms and jumping, slapping hands, even rubbing the backs of their heads together; and then, bent double, with the top half of the body hanging loosely down, long hair flopping into the face, they dragged themselves round practically on their knees. When the band played a rumba, the dancers went into wild ecstasy. They all leaped around and mumbled the chorus in English. The band played wilder and wilder numbers; none of the players was sitting any longer, they all 'jitterbugged' on the stage like wild animals. Frequently boys could be observed dancing together, without exception with two cigarettes in the mouth, one in each corner . . .

With the ban on public functions, the swing movement shifted to informal groupings where, naturally, its character became more sharply defined. Swing clubs sprang up particularly in big cities: Hamburg, Kiel, Berlin, Stuttgart, Frankfurt, Dresden, Halle and Karlsruhe. Their members were predominantly middle-class adolescents with enough schooling to be able to use the English lyrics and bits of foreign slang. Like the Edelweiss Pirates, who had used German-language hits against the National Socialists, so the *Swing-Jugend* picked up mainstream jazz that was quite permissible in variety shows and dances and radicalised it: they made it into an emblem of a youth culture that rejected the Hitler-Youth ideals, stripped it of its domesticated dance-floor character and favoured hotter varieties of what in Nazi parlance was termed 'negro music'. Dance music gave way to hot jazz; steps as learned in dancing classes gave way to free, spontaneous rhythmic movement, erect posture and tidy dress gave way to 'jitterbugging', hair 'down to the collar' (to quote the same Hitler-Youth report) and a cult of 'slovenliness' and 'sleaziness'.

The characteristics of the swing scene reflected the difference in social background between the offspring of the urban middle class and the working-class Edelweiss Pirates. The latter met on street corners and in parks, outside the confines of the parental home yet within a neighbourhood territory. The swing boys and girls had the money, clothes and status to be seen at bourgeois city-centre night clubs, as well as homes that were large enough for them to indulge in their 'jitterbugging' and 'sleaziness' when their elders were out. They had gramophone records; they could get hold of chic English-looking clothes.

A relaxed regime in their parents' houses, or lack of night-time supervision offered ample opportunity for gaining sexual experience. Reporting about the swing groups, the Nazi authorities stressed the incidence of promiscuity, group sex, sexual intercourse involving minors and, above all, unabashed pleasure in sexuality which was denounced as moral degeneracy. The wording and tone of such internal reports as a rule said more about their authors and readers than about the actual behaviour of the adolescents. Things were taken too literally that perhaps were only bragging; isolated 'incidents' were generalised. Even this caveat, however, does not alter the fact that the sexual behaviour of these adolescents clearly deviated from National Socialist acceptability.

The swing youth were not anti-fascist in a political sense—their behaviour was indeed emphatically anti-political—but both Nazi slogans and traditional nationalism were of profound indifference to them. They sought their counter-identity in what they saw as the 'slovenly' culture of the wartime enemies, England and America. They accepted Jews and 'half-Jews' into their groups—another outrage for the Nazis—and gave ovations to visiting bands from Belgium and Holland.

The very disgust shown by the authors of the Nazi reports and their dramatisation of events indicate that Nazi officialdom felt attacked at the heart of its concept of itself and of the State. This is the only way, too, to explain the reaction of Heinrich Himmler, who wanted to put the 'ringleaders' of the swing movement into concentration camps for at least two or three years of beatings, punitive drill and forced labour.

These alternative forms of social behaviour within the Third Reich show that considerable sections of the younger generation held themselves aloof from National Socialism. When the Hitler Youth seemed to have established itself officially, with compulsory membership, it met with apathy and rejection on the part of many adolescents, who were constantly to be found along the border line between passive and active insubordination. Despite various forms of repression, opposition groupings seem also to have been attractive to many adolescents who did not actually join them.

Furthermore, the everyday experience of National Socialism, for both working-class and middle-class youth, and their need to give expression to their identity, ran so contrary to what National Socialist ideology and its encrusted organisational structures had to offer, that the creation by young people of their own cultural identity and alternative styles naturally made itself apparent above all in the realm that was important for their age group: namely, leisure. These subcultures demonstrated that National Socialism, even after years in power, still did not have a complete grip on German society: indeed, sections of society slipped increasingly from its grasp the more it was able to perfect its formal means of organisation and repression.

The two central projects of National Socialist social policy—the abolition of class division through feelings of belonging to a 'racial community' (*Volksgemeinschaft*) and the smashing of the perceived threat to traditional values from modernity and internationalism—seem to have run aground even before the end of the Third Reich loomed ahead with military defeat.

National Socialism unintentionally paved the way for these manifestations of modern youth culture. Its power was sufficient largely to destroy the traditional forms of working-class and middle-class cultures. In their places, however, National Socialism could offer only military discipline, an anachronistic ideology and a stifling bureaucracy. The National Socialist blueprint for a future order failed to shape society in its image.

HITLER AND THE GERMANS

Ian Kershaw

FOR almost a decade after 1933, Hitler enjoyed a remarkable degree of popularity among the great majority of the German people. However dramatic and spectacular his political career, concentration on Hitler's character and personality—in some respects bizarre, in others downright mediocre and wholly unpleasant—can nevertheless do little to explain the magnetism of his popular appeal. Nor can his extraordinary impact on the German people in these years be accounted for satisfactorily by seeing in Hitler's personal *Weltanschauung* (notably in his obsessions with the 'Jewish Question' and with *Lebensraum*) a mirror image of the motivation of Nazism's mass following. Recent research has done much to qualify such assumptions, suggesting too that even deep into the period of the dictatorship itself Hitler's own ideological fixations had more of a symbolic than concrete meaning for most Nazi supporters.

What seems necessary, therefore, is an examination not of Hitler's personality, but of his popular image—how the German people saw their leader: the 'Hitler myth'. The Hitler myth was a double-sided phenomenon. On the one hand, it was a masterly achievement in image-building by the exponents of the new techniques of propaganda, building upon notions of 'heroic' leadership widespread in right-wing circles long before Hitler's rise to prominence. On the other hand, it has to be seen as a reflection of 'mentalities', value-systems, and socio-political structures which conditioned the acceptance of a 'Superman' image of political leadership. Both the active manufacture of Hitler's public image and the receptivity to it by the German people need, therefore, to be explored.

Images of 'heroic' leadership were already gaining ground in populist-nationalist circles of the German Right in the late nineteenth century. Their inclusion as a growing force in the political culture of the Right in the Kaiser's Germany (and there are parallels in pre-fascist Italy, which later gave rise to the cult of the *Duce*) was largely shaped by three interlinked factors: the social and political disruption accompanying a simultaneous transition to nation-state, constitutional government (if strongly authoritarian in character), and industrialised society; the deep fragmentation of the political system (reflecting fundamental social cleavages); and, not least, the spread of a chauvinistic-imperialist ideology clamouring for a rightful 'place in the sun' for Germany, a 'have-not' nation.

Growing disappointment on the populist Right with Wilhelm II promoted notions of a 'People's Kaiser' who, embodying strength and vitality, would crush Germany's internal enemies and, at the expense of inferior peoples, would provide the new nation with greatness and would win an empire for 'a people without living space'.

The extreme glorification of military values before and especially during the First World War, and the Right's shock and trauma at defeat, revolution, and the victory of the hated Social Democrats, promoted the extension and partial transformation of 'heroic' leadership images in the 1920s. Following the abdication of the Kaiser and the end of the old political order, ideal leadership was envisaged as being embodied in a man from the people whose qualities would reflect struggle, conflict, the values of the trenches. Hard, ruthless, resolute, uncompromising, and radical, he would destroy the old privilege- and class-ridden society and bring about a new beginning, uniting the people in an ethnically pure and socially harmonious 'national community'. The extreme fragmentation of Weimar politics kept such visions alive on the nationalist and *völkisch* Right. And by the early 1930s, perceptions of the total failure of Weimar democracy and mortal crisis of the entire political system allowed the image to move from the wings of politics to centre stage. By then, one man in particular was making a claim—accepted by increasing numbers of people—that he alone could re-awaken Germany and restore the country's greatness. This was Adolf Hitler, the leader of the Nazis.

Within the Nazi Party, the beginnings of a personality cult around Hitler go back to 1922–3, when some party members were already comparing him with Napoleon or describing him as Germany's Mussolini. Of course, Hitler only gradually established an unchallengeable authority within the party, initially having to contend with some powerful factions of opposition. And although his own concept of leadership was already becoming more 'heroic' in the year before his Putsch attempt, it was only during imprisonment following its failure that he came to believe that he himself was Germany's predestined great leader. During the following years in which the Nazis were little more than a minor irritant in German politics, the Hitler myth was consciously built up within the movement as a device to integrate the party, to fend off leadership challenges, and to win new members. The introduction in 1926 of a compulsory *'Heil Hitler'* fascist-style greeting and salute among party members was an outward sign of their bonds with their leader. Pseudo-religious imagery and fanciful rhetoric so ludicrous that it even occasionally embarrassed Hitler became commonplace in references to the leader in party publications.

Before 1930, the nascent Führer cult around Hitler found an echo among at most a few hundred thousand followers. But with the Nazi Party's breakthrough in the 1930 election (which brought it 18.3 per cent of the vote), the Führer cult ceased to be merely the property of a fanatical fringe party. The potential was there for its massive extension, as more and more Germans saw in Nazism—symbolised by its leader—the only hope for a way out of gathering crisis. Those now surging to join the Nazi party were often already willing victims of the Hitler myth. Not untypical was the new party member who wrote that after hearing Hitler speak for the first time, 'there was only one thing for me, either to win with Adolf Hitler or to die for him. The personality of the Führer had me totally in its spell'. Even for the vast majority of the German people who did not share such sentiments, there was the growing feeling—encouraged by Hitler's profile even in the non-Nazi press—that Hitler was not just another politician, that he was a party leader extraordinary, a man towards whom one could not remain neutral. He polarised feelings between bitter hatred and ecstatic devotion, but he could no longer be ignored, or shrugged off as a political nonentity.

For the thirteen million Germans who voted Nazi in 1932, Hitler symbolised—chameleon-like—the various facets of Nazism which they found appealing. In his public portrayal, he was a man of the people, his humble origins emphasising the rejection of privilege and the sterile old order in favour of a new, vigorous, upwardly-mobile society built upon strength, merit, and achievement. He was seen as strong, uncompromising, ruthless. He embodied the triumph of true Germanic virtues—courage, manliness, integrity, loyalty, devotion to the cause—over the effete decadence, corruption, and effeminate weakness of Weimar society. Above all, he represented 'struggle'—as the title of his book *Mein Kampf* advertised: struggle of the 'little man' against society's 'big battalions', and mortal struggle against Germany's powerful internal and external enemies to assure the nation's future. More prosaically, for the many still less convinced, he headed a huge mass movement which, given the weak and divided Weimar parties, seemed to offer the only way out of all-embracing crisis.

Still, not one German in two cast a vote for Hitler's party in the March election of 1933—held five weeks after Hitler had been appointed Chancellor in an atmosphere of national euphoria coupled with terroristic repression of the Left. Most Germans remained either hostile to, or unconvinced by, their new 'people's Chancellor', as the Nazi press dubbed him. Within the diehard ranks of the persecuted socialist and Communist Left, of course, the hatred of Hitler and all he stood

Two glimpses of Berlin life during the 1930s.

1. (*Above*) Christmas market in the Berlin Lustgarten in 1934.

2. (*Right*) Berlin's showpiece boulevard, Unter den Linden, decorated with eagles and swastikas shortly before the outbreak of war in 1939. The photo shows the famous Café Kranzler at the corner of Unter den Linden and Friedrichstrasse.

3. (*Above*) Workers assemble along the banks of the River Main to begin work on the first Autobahn, September 1933.

4. (*Left*) The propaganda image of the Autobahn: a picnic at the side of the Autobahn between Berlin and Stettin (today's Szczecin).

5. A posed family scene from 1937. The original caption to the photo read: 'The SA uniform is ironed.'

Kraft durch Freude

Auch Du kannst jetzt reisen!

Mass tourism in the Third Reich.

6. (*Left*) The politics of leisure—a poster of the 'Strength through Joy' organisation, encouraging Germans to save up for travel. The caption at the bottom reads: 'Now you too can travel!'

7. (*Below*) Members of a butchers' singing association from North Hessen enjoy an outing along the Rhine in the mid-1930s.

Ein Volk, ein Reich, ein Führer!

The production of the Hitler myth.

8. (*Left*) 'One People, One Reich, One Leader.' This poster, dating from 1938, could be found in countless government offices and schools.

9. (*Below*) The public face of the Führer, a man who loved children and dogs.

10. Photos from a book on youth criminality and threats to the moral health of the nation's youth, published in 1941.

Zwei Swingtypen
('Two swing types')

,,englisch—lässig"
('English—casual')

Swingjugend bei Hot-Musik
('Swing youth with hot music')

11. A youth gang, the Navajos from Cologne, arrested during Easter 1940.

12. Twelve young Edelweiss Pirates are publicly hanged in the working-class district of Cologne-Ehrenfeld in 1944.

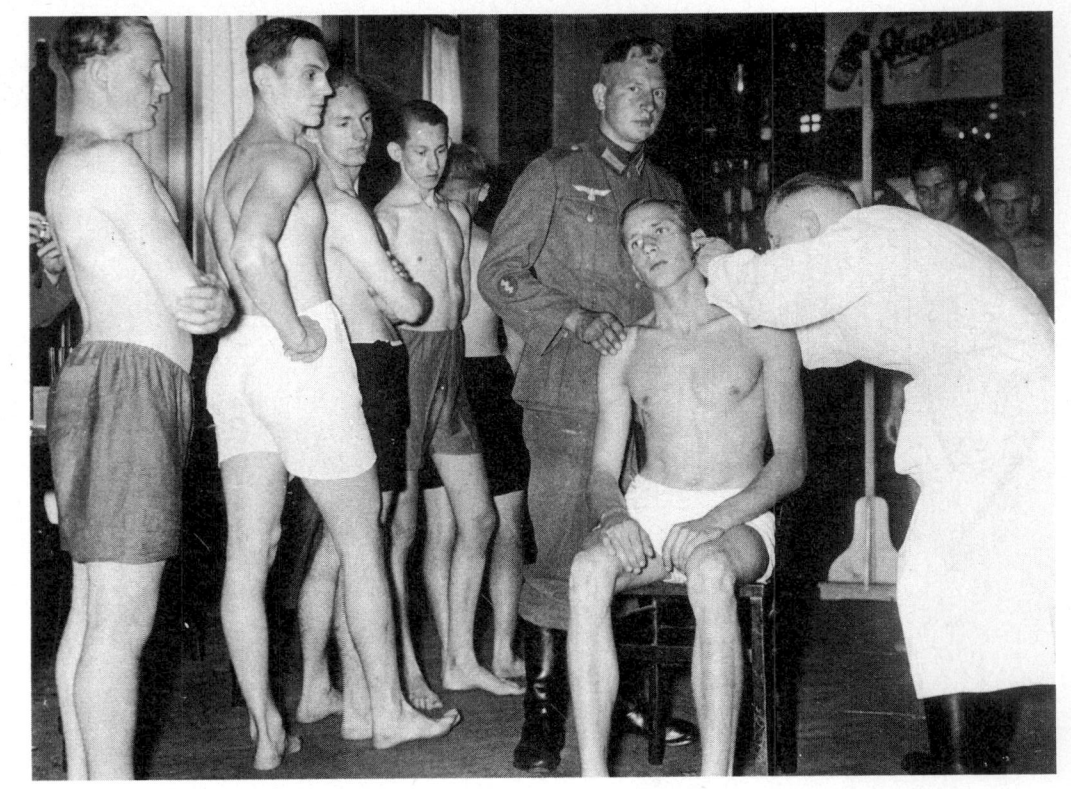

13. For millions, daily life in Nazi Germany was life in uniform. The photo shows conscripts born in 1915 and 1916 undergoing medical tests in Berlin in June 1937.

for—which in many respects was accurately foreseen—was implacable. In Catholic quarters, deep suspicions lingered about the anti-Christian tendencies of Nazism—though there was already a growing readiness to distance Hitler himself from the 'dangerous elements' in his movement. And bourgeois circles continued to see in Hitler the social upstart and vulgar demagogue, mouthpiece of the hysterical masses, the head of a party containing some wild and threatening elements—but a man, with all his faults, who could have his uses for a time. Attitudes towards Hitler in early 1933 varied greatly, therefore, and were often heatedly negative.

Three factors at least have to be taken into account in explaining how, nevertheless, the Führer cult could, within a strikingly short time, extend its hold to wide sections of the population, and eventually to the overwhelming majority of Germans. Of crucial significance was the widespread feeling that the Weimar political system and leadership was utterly bankrupt. In such conditions, the image of a dynamic, energetic, 'youthful' leader offering a decisive change of direction and backed by an army of fanatical followers was not altogether unattractive. Many with grave doubts were prepared to give Hitler a chance. And compared with the pathetic helplessness of his predecessors as Chancellor, the apparent drive and tempo of government activity in the months after he took office seemed impressive.

Secondly, the gross underestimation of Hitler again paved the way for at first reluctant or condescending, and then whole-hearted, enthusiasm for the way he apparently mastered within such a short time the internal political situation which had seemed beyond the capabilities of an upstart rabble-rouser. Thirdly, and most importantly, Hitler embodied an already well-established, extensive ideological consensus which also embraced most of those, except the Left, who had still not given him their vote in March 1933. Its chief elements were virulent anti-Marxism and the perceived need for a powerful counter to the forces of the Left; deep hostility towards the failed democratic system and a belief that strong, authoritarian leadership was necessary for any recovery; and a widespread feeling, even extending to parts of the Left, that Germany had been badly wronged at Versailles, and was threatened by enemies on all sides. This pre-existing wide consensus offered the potential for strong support for a national leader who could appear to offer absolute commitment, personal sacrifice, and selfless striving in the cause of inner unity and outward strength.

By 1933, Nazi propaganda had been highly successful in establishing 'charismatic authority' as the organisational premise of the Nazi Party, and then in portraying Hitler to Nazi sympathisers as not just another party leader, but as *the* Leader for whom the nation had been waiting—a man of incomparably different stature to contemptible party politicians. The most important propaganda step now remained to be taken: the conversion, for the 'majority of the majority' that had still not supported Hitler in March 1933, of his image from that of leader of the Nazi Movement to that of national leader.

Given the fact that Nazi propaganda now enjoyed a virtual monopoly within Germany, and that those taking a less than favourable view of Hitler's qualities were now incarcerated or silenced by fear and repression, the scene was set for the rapid establishment by the end of 1934 of the full-blown Führer cult of an almost deified national leader. No doubt many Germans found the extremes of the now omnipresent Hitler cult nauseating. But they were for the most part coming to accept that Hitler was no ordinary head of government. Above all, one could not ignore his 'achievements': 'order' had been restored; unemployment was falling rapidly; the economy was picking up strongly; Germany was beginning to stand up for itself again in the world. The record seemed to speak for itself.

By 1935, Hitler could be hailed in the Nazi press—and there was by now hardly any other press to speak of inside Germany—as the 'Symbol of the Nation' who, having struggled as an 'ordinary worker' to establish Germany's 'social freedom', had now, as a one-time ordinary 'Front soldier', re-established Germany's 'national freedom'—a reference to the recent reassertion of German military sovereignty. The message being conveyed was that people and nation found their identity, their 'incarnation', as it was put, in the person of the Führer. To this weight placed upon Hitler's 'achievements', Goebbels added the pathos of the human qualities of the Führer: his simplicity and modesty, toil and endeavour for his people, mastery of all problems facing the nation, toughness and severity, unshakeable determination though flexibility of method in the pursuit of far-sighted goals. With all this went the intense loneliness and sadness of a man who had sacrificed all personal happiness and private life for his people. This extraordinary catalogue of personal virtues—making the 'human' Hitler almost inhuman in the degree of his perfection—was set alongside the political genius of the Führer as a human counterpart to the image of the lofty, distant statesman. It amounted to almost a mirror of contemporary bourgeois values—characteristics with which almost everyone could find some point of association.

Difficult though it is to evaluate, evidence of the receptivity to this image—drawn both from sources from within the regime and those hostile to the Nazi system—lends strong support to Goebbels's claim in 1941 that the creation of the Hitler myth had been his greatest propaganda achievement. The powerfully integrative force of Hitler's massive popularity seems undeniable. Goebbels might have added, however, that the way had been paved for him by the constant exposure to rabid chauvinist-imperialist values pumped into the population for decades by a stridently nationalist press (excepting the publications of the Left) and by a variety of forms of 'socialisation' in schools, the bourgeois youth movement, the army, and an entire panoply of 'patriotic' clubs, leagues, and associations.

Of course, the political culture was far from a unitary one, and not all Germans were affected. As is well known, the socialist subculture remained relatively immune. Those 'schooled' in the traditions of the Socialist and Communist parties continued throughout the Third Reich to be the least susceptible to the appeal of the Hitler myth. To a lesser extent, the Catholic subculture was also resistant to the full extremes of the Führer cult, though strong traditions of authoritarianism and especially endemic anti-Marxism allowed for substantial inroads. Clearly, therefore, Hitler's popularity was far from complete, the Führer cult far from uniform in its impact. However, detailed examination of an extensive mass of sources relating to the formation of popular opinion and attitudes in the Third Reich suggests at least seven significant bases of the Hitler myth which can be singled out.

Firstly, Hitler was seen as the embodiment of strong and, where necessary, ruthless enforcement of 'law and order'—the representative of 'popular justice', the voice of the 'healthy sentiment of the people'. An example can be seen in the great gains in popularity which accrued to him in spring 1933 as a result of the brutal Nazi onslaught on the Left, 'clearing away' the Socialist and Communist 'enemies of the State'. Even more spectacular as an illustration is the extraordinary boost to Hitler's popularity following the ruthless massacre of members of his own Movement—the leaders of the highly unpopular SA—in June 1934. In reality, the purge of the SA leadership served to crush a destabilising element in the regime and further the power-political ambitions of the army and the SS. But none of this was reflected in Hitler's image following the purge. As even opponents of the regime acknowledged, Hitler's bloodletting was hugely popular, welcomed as a blow struck for law and order—'popular justice' eradicating corruption and immorality within the movement. The propagated image of a leader upholding public morality corresponded closely with commonly-held values and prejudices—for instance, in the condemnation of rowdiness and disorder, venal corruption and homosexuality. In what was a complete inversion of reality, Hitler was seen to be signalling a triumph for values associated with 'normality'.

Secondly, Hitler was seen as representing the national interest, putting the nation first before any particularist cause and wholly detached from any personal, material, or selfish motives. Crucial to this image was the way, after 1933, in which propaganda succeeded in isolating Hitler from the growing unpopularity of the Nazi Party itself. The wholly positive resonance of the portrayal of Hitler, the national leader, contrasted vividly with the sullied reputation of party functionaries, the 'little Hitlers', whose corruption and greed, jumped-up arrogance and high-handedness, pettiness and hypocrisy, were a daily scandal. And whereas the local party officials bore the brunt of extensive and real daily discontent, Hitler's popularity was cushioned by the myth that he was being kept in the dark about the misdeeds of his underlings, was unaware of the just complaints of his people.

Without at least the prospect of an improved living standard, the extent of the effective integration produced by the Hitler myth would have been difficult to achieve. A third, extremely important, component of the perceived Führer image was, therefore, that of the architect and creator of Germany's 'economic miracle' of the 1930s. Part of the apologetic of the post-war era was, of course, that despite his 'mistakes', Hitler had revamped the economy, rid Germany of unemployment, and built the motorways. This is itself testimony to the penetrating and enduring features of this aspect of the contemporary Hitler image. Certainly, by 1939 it was difficult to deny that economic conditions in Germany, for whatever reasons, had improved dramatically since the Depression era. However, more than in any other sphere, perceptions of Hitler's image in the context of economic and social policy were determined by experiences which divided for the most part along class lines.

The working class remained the social grouping least

impressed by the 'economic miracle' and *relatively* immune to the image of Hitler as the creator of Germany's striking new prosperity. After all, with their own standard of living pinned down to Depression levels in the years 1933–6, most industrial workers saw no particular reason to offer marked signs of gratitude to the Führer. Through repression and intimidation, low wages, and longer hours, the 'economic miracle', as most realised, was being carried out on their own backs. Nevertheless, as the underground worker resistance was forced to admit, Hitler undoubtedly did gain some popularity among workers for 'his' work creation and the economic recovery which 'he' had brought about. And in the first years of the Third Reich in particular, the 'socialist' aspect of the Hitler image also struck a chord among many of the poorer Germans who were recipients of the 'Winter Aid'. Even so, on the whole it appears that the image of the economic miracle-worker, the restorer of Germany's prosperity, had its greatest appeal among those sectors of the population who benefited most from the economic boom of the rearmament period: the middle class, who, despite their unceasing grumbling, continued to provide the main base of support for the regime and devotion to Hitler until at least the middle of the war.

Fourthly, in matters affecting established institutions and traditions, Hitler was seen as a 'moderate', opposed to the radical and extreme elements in the Movement. An obvious example is the 'church struggle'. Whenever fundamental institutions or basic traditional props of both major Christian denominations were under attack—as in the Nazi attempt in 1934 to abolish surviving Protestant bishoprics with a firm tradition of independence, or to remove crucifixes, the symbol of Christianity itself, from Catholic schoolrooms in 1936 and again in 1941, Hitler was looked to as the defence against the 'wild elements' in the party.

His apparent non-involvement in, or aloofness from, the bitter conflicts, before finally intervening to end the disturbance—put down to party radicals and the 'new heathen-ism' associated above all with Rosenberg—and 'restore order', left Hitler's standing among churchgoers relatively unscathed, despite the slump in popularity of the party. Grotesque as it seems, Hitler himself continued to be widely regarded as a God-fearing and deeply religious man. Even church leaders with a reputation for hostility to Nazism were persuaded of his sin-cerity, belief in God, and acceptance of the role of Christianity and the churches. Their public avowals of obedience to the Führer and recognition of his leadership and achievements played no small part in helping to give legitimation to the Hitler myth.

Fanatical commitment to uncompromising and ruthless action against the 'enemies of the people' was a fifth crucial component of Hitler's image. But he was regarded as condon-ing only lawful, 'rational' action, not the crude violence and public brutalities of the party's distasteful 'gutter' elements. No one could have been left in any doubt, for instance, of Hitler's fanatical anti-Semitism and determination to exclude Jews from German society. And at the beginning of his career, anti-Semitism had been a key note of almost all his speeches and must have been a dominant component of his popular image among early converts to Nazism. However, during the period of the party's major electoral successes, anti-Semitism appears to have featured less prominently in Hitler's public addresses, and was less important as an electoral drawing card than has often been presumed—tending mainly to function as a general touchstone for other propaganda themes.

After 1933, Hitler was extremely careful to avoid public association with the generally unpopular pogrom-type anti-Semitic outrages, particularly of course following the nation-wide 'Crystal Night' pogrom in November 1938. In the years when his popularity was soaring to dizzy heights, moreover, Hitler's public pronouncements on the 'Jewish Question' were less numerous than might be imagined, and, while certainly hate-filled, were usually couched in abstract generalities in association with western plutocracy or Bolshevism. In these terms, bolstering the passive anti-Semitism already widespread among the German people and lending support to 'legal' measures—for the most part popular—excluding Jews from German society and the economy, Hitler's hatred of the Jews was certainly an acceptable component of his popular image, even if it was an element 'taken on board' rather than forming a centrally important motivating factor for most Germans. Even during the war, when his vitriolic public onslaughts on the Jews came far more frequently and contained dire allusions to their physical extermination, the signs are that this was not a centrally formative factor shaping attitudes towards Hitler among the German people.

Sixthly, Hitler's public profile in the arena of foreign affairs stood in stark contrast to reality. He was commonly seen here as a fanatical upholder of the nation's just rights to territory 'robbed' from Germany in the peace settlement after the First World War, a rebuilder of Germany's strength, and a statesman of genius—to which his astounding run of diplomatic coups seemed to offer ample testimony. Amid the widespread, deep fears of another war, he was also, astonishingly, seen by many as a 'man of peace' who 'would do everything he could to settle things peacefully' (as one then youthful observer later came to describe her feelings at the time)—a defender of German rights, not a racial-imperialist warmonger working towards a 'war of annihilation' and limitless German conquest. Hitler's imposing series of 'triumphs without bloodshed' directed at 'peace with honour'—tearing up the Versailles settlement, winning back the Saar, restoring 'military sovereignty', recovering the Rhineland, uniting Austria with Germany, and bringing the Sudetenland 'home into the Reich'—won him support in all sections of the German people and unparalleled popularity, prestige, and acclaim.

Finally, there is Hitler's image, when war came, as the

military strategist of genius, outwitting Germany's enemies in an unbelievable run of Blitzkrieg victories, culminating in the taking of France within four weeks when a generation earlier four years had not been enough. Even after the war started to turn sour for Germany in the winter of 1941–2, the unpopularity of the party and its despised representatives at home continued for a time to stand in stark contrast to the image of the Führer's devotion to duty in standing with his soldiers at the Front. However, according to Max Weber's model, 'charismatic leadership' could not survive lack of success. And indeed, as 'his' astonishing run of victories turned gradually but inexorably into calamitous defeat, the tide of Hitler's popularity first waned rather slowly, then ebbed sharply. The decline accelerated decisively following the catastrophe of Stalingrad, a defeat for which Hitler's personal responsibility was widely recognised.

The Hitler myth was now fatally flawed. In the face of defeats, personal losses, misery, and sacrifice, the earlier successes began to be seen in a new light. Hitler was now increasingly blamed for policies which had led to war. His much vaunted strong will, resolution, unshakeable determination, and absolute fanaticism were regarded more and more not as attributes but as the main stumbling blocks to the longed-for peace. With no more successes to proclaim, Hitler was now reluctant even to speak to the German people. The new image put out by Goebbels of Hitler as a latter-day Frederick the Great—distant majesty finally triumphant in the face of extreme adversity—symbolised the growing gulf.

Important reserves of popularity remained to the end. Hatred of the Allies prompted by terror bombing campaigns partially benefited Hitler and the regime for a while; some temporary vain hopes were placed in the Führer's promises of new weapons which would accomplish the desired 'retaliation'; a short-lived upsurge of support and proclamation of loyalty followed the attempt on his life in July 1944—an indication that a successful coup might have encountered a new version of the 'stab-in-the-back' legend; and surprisingly large numbers of prisoners-of-war in the west continued till the end to avow their belief in Hitler. But the potency of the Hitler myth had vanished. Eloquent commentary on this is a report on a remembrance ceremony at the war memorial in the little Bavarian alpine town of Markt Schellenberg on March 11th, 1945:

When the leader of the Wehrmacht unit at the end of his speech for the remembrance called for a *'Sieg Heil'* for the Führer, it was returned neither by the Wehrmacht present, nor by the *Volkssturm,* nor by the spectators of the civilian population who had turned up. This silence of the masses had a depressing effect, and probably reflects better than anything the attitudes of the people.

Unquestionably, the adulation of Hitler by millions of Germans who may otherwise have been only marginally committed to the Nazi ideology, or party, was a crucial element of political integration in the Third Reich. Without this mass base of support, the high level of plebiscitary acclamation, which the regime could repeatedly call upon to legitimise its actions and to take the wind out of the sails of the opposition, is unthinkable. It also enabled the specifically Nazi élite to free itself from dependence upon the support of traditional conservative ruling groups, thereby boosting the autonomy of the 'wild men' in the Movement. Without the degree of popular backing which Hitler was able to command, the drive, dynamism, and momentum of Nazi rule could hardly have been sustained.

The Führer cult necessarily influenced the relations of the Nazi leadership itself with Hitler, as well as those of the traditional ruling élites. Inevitably, it surrounded Hitler with toadies, flatterers, and sycophants, shielding him from rational criticism or genuine debate, and bolstered increasing detachment from reality. Nor could Hitler himself remain impervious to the extraordinary cult which had been created around him and which came to envelop him. His own person gradually became inseparable from the myth.

Hitler had to live out more and more the constructed image of omnipotence and omniscience. And the more he succumbed to the allure of his own Führer cult and came to believe in his own myth, the more his judgement became impaired by faith in his own infallibility and guidance 'by providence', enabling him to 'go his way with the certainty of a sleep-walker'. His room for manoeuvre now became restricted by his own need to protect the Hitler myth and sustain his prestige, aware as he was that if Nazism lost its forward momentum and stagnation set in, Hitler's own popularity and the mass base of the regime's support would be fatally undermined. To this extent, it has been claimed with some justification, that 'Hitler well understood his own function, the role which he had to act out as "Leader" of the Third Reich', that he 'transformed himself into a function, the function of Führer'.

THE NAZI STATE RECONSIDERED

Michael Geyer

THE vices which despotism engenders are precisely those which equality fosters. These two things mutually and perniciously complete and assist each other. Equality places men side by side, unconnected by any common tie; despotism raises barriers to keep them asunder: the former predisposes them not to consider their fellow-creatures, the latter makes general indifference a sort of virtue. Despotism then, which is at all times dangerous, is most particularly to be feared in democratic ages.

Alexis de Tocqueville, *Democracy in America* (vol. II, chapter iv)

UNFETTERED competition is one of the least understood features of the National Socialist regime, although it is one of the most discussed. Political historians have long debunked the myth of the National Socialist State as a totalitarian and rationally organised modern Leviathan. More recently, historians have been fascinated by the rampant competition, even chaos, of Nazi institutions. At the same time, social historians have come to regard as a major aspect of the National Socialist regime not the ideological infiltration of Nazi doctrine among the German people as though it were a new catechism, but the increasing pressures of competitive behaviour among social groups and individuals that reshaped private and public life, within the family no less than on the shop floor.

National Socialism replaced the hard driving, entrepreneurial, 'economic man' with a new breed of *compradores* who craftily exploited the chances of improvement and upward mobility provided by an expanding Third Reich. Their main pursuits were not economic or productive but 'political', using the powers of domination and subjugation that were provided by the State—starting with the repression of trade unions and the seizure of their property and the exclusion of Jews from public life and continuing in the wars of plunder and extortion which reached their zenith in the war against the Soviet Union.

All this has been fairly well described, but little understood. Historians, like most people, prefer to keep State and society, men and women, production and destruction neatly apart, and have very distinct ideas about what should and should not be considered modern. German and English historians both stop short of the notion of a State's institutions as the main arena of competition, although their reasons differ. The Germans imagine a well-organised and smooth-functioning State machine in which institutions not only fit together but, by functioning so well, also further the common good. English historians, on the other hand, come from a tradition that views the State or, more generally, the political sphere as an arena where a ruling class constitutes itself by establishing its claims to dominate through the consent of the subordinated classes.

Whichever way we approach it, the sprawling Nazi State with its many and diffuse institutions was different. Very clearly it became the site of pervasive competition between individuals and institutions for control over this power to dominate others; in turn this became the prerequisite for the wealth and the status of an institution. This competition increased in leaps and bounds with Nazi conquest. Those institutions and individuals who had the licence to plunder—and all too often the right to kill as well—ruled supreme. The SS and its sprawling empire under Himmler was the prime example of this kind of activity. This is what makes the Nazi regime so extraordinary and, at the same time, so difficult to understand. The Nazi State and the emerging Nazi society were not centred around production and maintaining its conditions, but around the ability to prey on other people and whole societies, much as industry preys on nature.

The consequence of this slash-and-burn approach to State activities was the collapse of the rule of law and of the rationality of bureaucratically organised domination. At the same time, the sphere of the State and the number of those who were employed by the State directly or indirectly expanded dramatically. This expansion, it should be noted, occurred in tandem with the intensification of terror and domination, beginning in 1933. At the zenith of the Second World War, in 1941, a State system had emerged in which literally hundreds of institutions were engaged in the project of dominating the defeated and occupied countries.

We are only slowly beginning to uncover the cumulative impact of these institutions, which fought each other tooth and nail. While we have a good sense of the plunder by the big 'machines'—the SS, the military, and industry—we still need to uncover the little privileges of 'Germans' over other 'races'. Thus we know a great deal about forced labour in Germany, but we know next to nothing about the behaviour of, for example, the administrators in the East—or about the increasingly inter-ethnic master–servant relations in the German countryside during the war. By the same token, a great deal is known about the 'Aryanisation' of industry and trade, but what happened to all the Jewish offices and houses, and to the property of Jewish families in Germany and Europe, say in Hamburg, Krakow, or Vienna? We really do not know.

However, a recent study on Passau has shown that even in the staunchly Catholic backwoods of Germany where Nazism never took a firm hold, the Third Reich could unleash a creed which broke through the old solidarities of the community and destroyed tolerance among people. Of all its vices, the ability of the National Socialist regime to separate and set human beings against one another in competition over plunder was the worst.

By destroying bonds of solidarity, by fostering the egotism of both individuals and institutions, and by applauding as strong and healthy those 'who have no sympathy for any but themselves', the National Socialist regime proceeded to create a State and a society which 'placed men side by side, unconnected by any common ties' (de Tocqueville). This competition did not centre around production or markets, but around terror and force, the capacity to impose one's will on others by means of physical coercion.

War was the natural extension of this violent system, and war in the National Socialist context took on a very special meaning. It has been appropriately called a *Weltanschauungskrieg*, an ideological war. This kind of war happened not only to be Hitler's main and ultimate goal; it was also the centrepiece of the reconstruction of German society and the German State around domination. Ideological war was the product neither of old-fashioned interest-politics nor of atavistic sentiments. Rather it was fought in order to create and maintain a State and a society in which German individuals and institutions could share in the domination of others.

If we consider war, and ideological war at that, as the focus of the National Socialist State, this may shed some light on the initial observation about the chaotic and competitive nature of Nazi rule.

It is true that the business of governing in the Third Reich was transformed into competitive interaction between power-holders and their institutions. There was no coherent system of government. Every institution carved out its own niche in an increasingly vicious struggle for influence and resources. Looking at the endless squabbles between them, it might indeed be surmised that the Nazi State was chaotic.

Even worse, the sharp divisions between State, economy, and society became lost under the impact of the competition. Industrial groups gained quasi-State authority and the difference between private and public ownership (one may think of the Hermann Goering Werke or of the holdings of German files in the occupied countries), became blurred. By the same token, the SS combined State institutions like the police with party institutions like the SD information service under one roof. Thus, a National Socialist State emerged that lacked a coherent

14. A street scene along Berlin's fashionable Kurfürstendamm in October 1941. The newspaper carries reports of the German Army's progress in the campaign against the Soviet Union. Living conditions in German cities did not really deteriorate until the massive Allied bombing campaigns began in 1942–3.

Pictures of life during the War in and around the village of Körle.

15. (*Above*) Visit from the Front, 1943.

16. (*Right*) Young women from Körle visit injured soldiers in hospital, 1942.

17. (*Below*) The local National Socialist Women's League after a collection for the victims of Allied bombing raids.

18. (*Top*) A roll-call at the Sachsenhausen concentration camp for political prisoners near Oranienburg (to the north of Berlin) in April 1933.

19. (*Bottom*) Tailors' workshop at the Sachsenhausen concentration camp in February 1941.

20. (*Above*) 1 April 1933: Nazi activists affix signs to the windows of Jewish shops, admonishing Germans not to buy from Jews. The one-day nationwide anti-Jewish boycott of April 1933 was not a great success, and was not repeated.

21. (*Right*) The sign, in front of allotments in Berlin, reads 'Jews are not welcome here'.

22. (*Left*) Cleaning up in Berlin after the pogrom of November 1938. One of the aspects of the pogrom which most upset Germans was scenes such as this, with property destroyed and broken glass littering the pavement.

23. (*Below*) Jewish men are rounded up in the city of Oldenburg to be taken to concentration camps after the November 1938 pogrom.

24. (*Top*) Jews are herded into a ghetto in the city of Kielce in occupied Poland, October 1939.

25. (*Bottom*) Women and children shortly before their trip to the gas chambers at Auschwitz.

26. Gypsies too were hunted, arrested, and murdered, both within Germany and in occupied Europe. This photo shows members of an arrested Gypsy family with German military police in occupied Russia during 1942.

27. Berlin, 1943: a mother, wearing a gas mask and a wet blanket as a protection against fire and smoke, during an air raid. In the background is a cinema; the film advertised is *Journey into the Past*.

centre and expanded beyond traditional boundaries to encompass parts of society and the economy.

Yet, as competitive as this system of National Socialist politics was and however blurred the line between State, society, and economy, this entity did not lack direction. To step back from the infighting and look at the system as a whole is to discover that the momentum of competition led in the direction of war. Many attribute this to Hitler personally, but this view is too simplistic an explanation for a modern despotic regime. Hitler's stature in the Third Reich did indeed rise and he was increasingly able to impose his 'goals', but his rise to predominance was a result rather than a precondition of the pervasive struggles over power, influence, and resources. A State system, built on plunder, could not but move in the direction of war—or it had to be thoroughly rebuilt.

However, we cannot leave it there; for National Socialist (and Hitler's) politics were not exhausted in following an institutional drive towards war. They wanted war and strove towards it. War was the means to reconstruct German society and the German State on the basis of conquest, subjugation, and annihilation. War was the goal of a process of social reconstruction that began with racial purification as the core of *Wiederwehrhaftmachung* (military preparedness) and was supposed to reach its climax with the anticipated domination of the Germans over other 'races'. This was the ideological programme. It was guided by the promise of domination for every German as part of a new 'master race' in a racist empire. While the big 'machines' fought it out among themselves, the Nazi leadership, and especially Hitler, never lost their populist touch. Both trajectories pointed towards war, and a racist war at that.

Competition over domination formed the material practice of the Third Reich. As de Tocqueville put it, 'a despot easily forgives his subjects for not loving him, provided they do not love each other'. The latter—love, trust, solidarity—indeed were in short supply among the Germans, and solidarity with the dominated became treason. Equality for all Germans in a new *Volksgemeinschaft*; freedom as participation in domination; egotism in the interest of the 'common good'—these were the ideological essentials of the Nazi State, which did not require that everyone become a Nazi as long as the National Socialist leadership could convince Germans of the benefits of racist rule.

Ideological politics were thus the promise of participation in the domination of others for one's own and the common German benefit. It was thus a peculiarly perverted system of participation; for while the Germans were not allowed to govern themselves, they were encouraged to dominate others. This was the National Socialist 'social contract' on which the State, with its competitive and predatory institutions, rested.

It is easy to be confused by the convenient 'mix-up' between Nazi propaganda and Nazi ideology. However, National Socialist ideology consisted neither of the bad political habits of the 'masses' nor the dreams produced in Dr Goebbels's celluloid factories. The special quality of National Socialist ideology consisted in its increasing concreteness with the approach and the conduct of war. Its very core, racist domination and annihilation, was its least debated and propagandised aspect, but it comprised the essence and the practice of politics in the Third Reich.

The National Socialist State system of competitive centres of power and a racist 'social contract' did not emerge overnight and it always remained tenuous, dependent both on the State's ability to reconcile the political interests of the institutional centres of power and the ability to create a new social contract through war. The National Socialist State was not the inevitable outcome of the seizure of power; nor did the Third Reich simply follow a path mapped out by Hitler. Rather, the conditions for ideological war and for the foundation of a new social contract were established in a series of struggles. There is, in other words, no linear progression in National Socialist rule, but a series of contested choices that made the Nazi State.

Conflicts over priorities were built into the coalition government that came to power in 1933. Least important in this coalition were the few conservative-bourgeois politicians who were quickly ousted or side-stepped. What counted was the power of industry and the military on the one hand, and of society mobilised in the National Socialist movement on the other. Not the parties which were quickly co-opted, but the autonomous powerblocks of industry and the military were the initial counterweights, but also the partners of the National Socialists. National Socialist leaders depended on industry in combatting unemployment and on the military to wage war, just as the latter depended on the National Socialist capacity to mobilise (and terrorise) people. As a result of the Nazi takeover, the powers of industry and the military expanded dramatically during 1933. But all attempts to fuse the National Socialist movement with the interests of industry and the military—as was tried in 1933 with the SA and the Wehrmacht and with the *Mittelstand* and industry—were frustrated, and failed. Both the attempt to bring together middle-class and industrial politics in the formation of a new corporate economy and the attempt to fuse paramilitary mobilisation with rearmament in a new hybrid military came to naught.

In fact the two sides came to a head-on collision in 1934 which the paramilitary and middle-class ideologies in the National Socialist movement lost. The *Reichswehr* became the dominant military force against and over the storm troopers just as industry pushed back *Mittelstand* demands. While the former demanded the subordination of the whole nation under the yoke of rearmament, the latter strove for efficiency and managerial control over the workforce. Both aims were as total in their scope as those of the National Socialists. They wanted to reorganise society in their own right to assure the smooth functioning of production and destruction. Even if the military and industry never fully succeeded, this constituted a most threatening challenge for the National Socialist leadership. In effect, they had to negate their past and the interests of their most dedicated followers in order to maintain their alliance with the military and industry on whom they depended in their short-term struggle against unemployment and their long-term objectives of waging war. The National Socialist leadership entered a most critical phase—and yet it survived and emerged stronger than before.

Nazi leaders all acted differently in this situation. The opportunistic Goering seized the first opportunity to join industry and the military as a third force through the Four-Year Plan, although he and the Plan remained unwelcome among the tycoons of the Ruhr. Nevertheless, Goering established his own power-base, centred around a military-industrial complex, that linked the air force with aeroplane manufacturers and chemical (especially synthetic petrol) industries, mainly IG Farben. Himmler concentrated on building his own apparatus of domination, which was the first in the Third Reich that lived entirely off the domination of others. In a series of crafty manoeuvres against his own National Socialist comrades (Röhm, Goering, Goebbels) and against State bureaucracies, he not only centralised policing, but also reforged the whole complex of 'domestic security' into a proselytising centre for ideological politics. Himmler's powerblock thus not only contained the political police, the Gestapo, but also the Race and Settlement Office which championed the reconstruction of German society along racist lines. It also developed its own 'resource' base by exploiting the victims of the Third Reich (concentration camp labour) and by seizing and controlling the property of those who were expelled from Germany. However, the survival of the Nazi leadership as a whole, and of Hitler in particular, was due to other factors.

Hitler's ideological base had always been somewhere else, and it was the clever preservation of this base by Goebbels which propelled Hitler to the centre of the stage without his having to make the decisions that industry and the military expected him to make. He was never a good mediator in the competition between his own leaders and between the institutions of the State and, from what is known, he did not care to perform well in this particular field. However, Hitler always retained his close ties with a German society which adored him despite the blunders of his entourage. While the party lost in credibility, Hitler's star rose thanks to the ceaseless propaganda campaigns of Goebbels. These bonds of loyalty and adoration that linked Hitler to society proved to be exceedingly important. While Hitler and the National Socialist regime did not fare very well in guiding the competition within the Nazi State, they continued to guarantee the conditions of production and destruction both internally and externally. In this capacity of establishing and maintaining a social contract, Hitler was desperately needed. The organisation of society for war or, for that matter, for production, could not have taken place without a growing Hitler myth, without Hitler's 'peace' initiatives, or without the dose of terror against those who did not opt for the emerging community of the Third Reich.

Had the Third Reich been an ordinary despotic regime, nothing further would have happened. The myth would have given way to disappointment and the dynamism of the regime would have petered out. There was the possibility of this kind of development all along, despite Goebbels's efforts. Yet at the first possible chance the National Socialist leadership proved that it was not an ordinary regime and that it was not ready to leave the social contract to propaganda and goodwill.

This chance arose in 1937–8 for complex reasons. Both the military and industry had over-reached themselves while neither of them had attained their goal. The military was still unable to fight a war, and industry continued to fear for profitability. They were in a genuine impasse, in which one side had to give. The military wanted more rearmament, industry a course of stability and profitability, and both were ready to pass the costs on to society. Hitler resisted this choice by pursuing a third, his own course. He drove towards a quick, even premature war—and not just any war, but ideological war. He used the impasse of 1937–8 to give the National Socialist social contract a substantive base through wars of exploitation and domination. He revived the quest for *Volksgemeinschaft* and *Lebensraum*. In 1938 the Nazi leadership succeeded in establishing the primacy of ideological politics. This was a most important change, for it shaped the quality of the wars to be fought. They were not simply fought in order to consolidate and to placate interests. They were fought as social wars in order to facilitate the reconstruction of German society.

This kind of war reached its apogee with the war against the Soviet Union in 1941. For that war linked the key aspects of ideological rule: exterminism and genocide and the reconstruction of German society as the superior 'race' over the subjugated peoples and nations came together in the planning and the implementation of 'Operation Barbarossa'. This campaign was ideology transformed into political, social, and military practice. In summer 1941, when the Soviet Union seemed to be defeated, a vision emerged of a German society, a National Socialist State, and a prosperous industry preying on subordinated peoples and resources, being protected by the SS against the resistance from within and by the Wehrmacht against the dangers from without. In 1941–2 the high watermark of the establishment of a racist social contract was reached. It is only appropriate that exactly at this point the preparations for a 'final solution', the annihilation of the Jewish people in occupied Europe, took shape.

However, this vision was destroyed in the very same winter by the tenacity of the Red Army. The ending of Blitzkrieg initiated a last phase in the development of a Nazi State. By 1941 the pendulum had begun to swing back to a more instrumental and functional organisation of society in the interests of production and destruction, while ideological politics were cramped into the annihilation campaign against Jews that escalated to its heights in 1941–2. Speer, and with him a corporate solution for the mobilisation of resources, gained the upper hand as far as the Germans were concerned. However, the main costs of the re-emergence of corporate power within the Nazi State and the reassertion of the imperatives of production in total war were still not paid by the Germans, but by forced labour, plunder, and starvation in occupied countries. This was and is Speer's legacy.

Underneath the pressures of war production organised in Speer's Ministry, alternatives were debated which proved to be more palatable in Germany and to the Germans. Many (like the future Minister of Economic Affairs and Chancellor Ludwig Ehrhard, but, intriguingly also the SS leader Ohlendorf who never gave up the vision of the reconstruction of German society) retained their dislike for Speer's corporatism with its quest for a clean and functional organisation of society in subordination to big industry. After all hopes for domination vanished in 1943, they began to debate alternative ways of mapping out a social contract—no longer on the basis of violence, but built around new economic policies. They aimed at achieving, in due course, high employment and a high standard of living as well as the creation of a European 'co-prosperity sphere', that is a zone of influence in which Germany would predominate, though not by force and violence, but due to its economic strength. They envisaged a new social contract, based not on the domination of others, but on a share in consumption in a revitalised and prospering European economy. Thus the basis for post-war reconstruction was laid during the war in response to the failure of the National Socialist State to establish a new and racist German order through war. However, the National Socialist State could not be reformed from within as some of the proponents of *Volkskapitalismus* had thought. The National Socialist regime had to be destroyed before a new social contract could be negotiated.

NAZI POLICY AGAINST THE JEWS

William Carr

FOR nearly twenty years after the collapse of Hitler's Reich first revealed the full horrors of the Holocaust it was widely supposed that genocide on this enormous scale must have been the last stage of a deliberate Nazi policy, a long-matured master plan which aimed all along at the physical annihilation of European Jewry. In the monolithic Nazi State where all power was allegedly concentrated in the Führer's hands, his vitriolic hatred of all things Jewish would have been sufficient on its own to explain the murder of six-and-a-half million Jews.

Not until the 1960s did historians generally accept that the Nazi State was no monolith but a mosaic of conflicting authorities bearing more resemblance to a feudal State, where great vassals were engaged in a ruthless power struggle to capture the person of the king who in his turn maintained his authority by playing one great lord off against another. The clear implication was that Nazi anti-Semitism must also have reflected the twists and turns of the power game and that Hitler's paranoid hatred of Jewry could only have been one—albeit most important—factor in a complex historical equation. Some historians now suggest that the Holocaust itself was not the final phase of a long-cherished plan but a piece of improvisation in an unexpected situation.

On one point all are agreed; Hitler and his followers were paranoid in their determination to turn Germany's half a million Jews into pariahs. Forming less than 1 per cent of the total population—and declining numerically—the Jews had resided in Germany for generations and had been for the most part assimilated into the life of the community. Only 20 per cent were the so-called 'Eastern Jews' who emigrated to Germany from the disturbed areas of Eastern Europe after the First

World War, still retained their distinctive Jewish garb and tended to live together in certain quarters of the great cities. Certainly Jews were prominent in the cultural and economic life of Berlin. And in certain professions there was a higher proportion of Jews than Aryans. For example, 17 per cent of all bankers were Jews—a much lower percentage than in the closing years of the nineteenth century; 16 per cent of all lawyers—but rarely was a judge Jewish; and 10 per cent of all doctors and dentists—but few held university or hospital posts. In the clothing and retail trades Jewish influence was pronounced. But in no way could it be argued that the Jews 'dominated' the cultural or economic life of Germany as the Nazis claimed. Nor were the Jews particularly wealthy; many of them were as poor as their Aryan neighbours, despite a well-earned reputation for hard work.

Nevertheless for rank-and-file Nazis the Jew had become a grotesque nightmare figure far removed from the reality of everyday life. In the viciously anti-Semitic literature pouring out from Nazi presses the Jew was denounced as the root cause of all Germany's ills and depicted as a sub-human figure burrowing away at the moral and economic foundations of the State and dedicated to the destruction of the whole world. In the cosmic confrontation between 'Good' and 'Evil' the Aryan race led by the German people was destined to save mankind from the horrors of the 'Jewish-Bolshevik' yoke, as exemplified by Russian Communism. No doubt anti-Semitism was a useful ploy to deflect the party's attention away from the Nazi leadership's partnership with the detested old order. But basically the crude and vicious anti-Semitism of Streicher's *Der Stürmer* was a psychological necessity for many party members, especially those in the Brownshirts and in Himmler's SS, who desperately needed 'outgroups'—including gypsies and Jehovah's Witnesses—on whom they could vent their personal frustrations.

However much Hitler sympathised with this crude and

visceral anti-Semitism, once he was in office he was obliged to try and contain rank-and-file outbursts in the interests of political stability, public order and economic recovery. Thus, when the Brownshirts went on the rampage after the Nazi electoral victory in March 1933 assaulting Jews and ransacking shops, he sought to canalise their energies through a centrally co-ordinated boycott of Jewish shops. Under pressure from President Hindenburg and Foreign Minister Neurath this boycott was limited to one day and never extended because of public apathy, foreign reactions and the danger of damaging a fragile economy. The reduction of unemployment had so high a priority that in July the Cabinet agreed to continue offering public contracts to Jewish firms. Similarly, when legislation was enacted in April to dismiss Jewish civil servants, Hitler had reluctantly to yield to Hindenburg's demand that all Jews appointed before 1914, all those who had fought in the First World War or whose fathers or sons had died in the war be exempt, a concession which partially emasculated the measure.

For the next two years the Jews enjoyed a period of relative freedom from persecution. This changed in the course of 1935. Certainly Hitler was in a much stronger position to give vent to his rabid anti-Semitism. Since Hindenburg's death he had been head of State and in 1934 had brought the Brownshirts sharply to heel. But it seems likely that a significant recrudescence of anti-Semitic agitation amongst rank-and-file Nazis forced him to give the Jews another turn of the screw.

Rank-and-file demands for a 'Jew-free economy' he had to resist as long as the contribution of Jewish firms to economic recovery was important. Where he did give way was in an area which, as the pornography of Streicher's *Der Stürmer* amply demonstrated, fascinated many anti-Semites: sexual relations between Jews and Gentiles. In the Law for the Protection of German Blood announced at the Party Rally in Nürnberg in September, marriage between them and sexual relations outside marriage were forbidden. Under the so-called Nürnberg

Laws Jews were also to be denied German citizenship and were forbidden to fly the German flag. It is significant that Hitler encountered no resistance from his civil servants. Indeed they positively welcomed legislation which by placing anti-Semitism on a sound legal foundation would prevent—they hoped—further disorderly street scenes so disturbing to tidy-minded bureaucrats.

Up to the end of 1937 Jews had managed to keep control of their businesses and could still use most of the amenities open to other Germans. Signs of a more radical anti-Semitic policy multiplied in the winter of 1937/8. At the Party Rally in September Hitler made an outspoken attack on Jews for the first time in two years. As the German economy moved into top gear, the big industrial concerns, eager to take over their Jewish competitors at knock-down prices, pressed the government to proceed to the 'Aryanisation' of the economy. To induce Jewish firms to sell out, Goering, plenipotentiary for the Four-Year Plan and the friend of big business, reduced their raw materials allocation and after the spring of 1938 they received no further public contracts. Following the *Anschluss* with Austria, Goering issued a decree ordering Jews to register all property above 5000 Marks in value and forbidding them to sell it without permission. In the summer of 1938 Jewish doctors, dentists and lawyers were forbidden to offer their services to Aryans. Even the names to be given Jewish children were specified in a new directive. Jews with other names had to add Israel or Sarah to them. Jews were now obliged to carry identity cards and from October all Jewish passports were stamped with the letter J.

After *Reichskristallnacht* (Night of broken glass) on November 9th–10th, 1938, the position of German Jewry deteriorated more rapidly still. On that night ninety-one Jews were murdered, 20,000 thrown into concentration camps, synagogues were burnt down all over Germany and thousands of Jewish shops vandalised (the broken glass littering the pavements gave its name to the incident) in an unprecedented outburst of savagery carried out by party activists and carefully orchestrated from Josef Goebbels's Propaganda Ministry. World opinion was profoundly shocked by the spectacle of a pogrom in a hitherto civilised country; the trade boycott on German goods intensified; and Franklin Roosevelt withdrew Ambassador Dodds from Berlin.

World opinion, alas, could do little to alleviate the plight of the Jews. A spate of discriminatory decrees were issued aimed at creating a 'Jew-free' economy. Jews were now forbidden to practice trades or to own shops or market stalls or manage businesses. Jewish shops, firms and real estate holdings were 'Aryanised'—that is compulsorily sold to Aryan competitors. In later decrees Jews were totally excluded from schools and universities, cinemas, theatres and sports facilities. In many cities, where of course the bulk of the Jewish population was resident, Jews were forbidden to enter designated 'Aryan' areas. This legislation was enforced zealously by local fanatics so that by the outbreak of war the Jew was well on the way to becoming the pariah in German society towards which the Nazi party had been working for so long.

The radicalisation of the regime's anti-Semitic policy on the eve of war cannot, however, be attributed simply and solely to Hitler's vindictive attitude but has to be seen against the political background. In the winter of 1937/8 as the pace of German foreign policy began to accelerate, the balance of power inside Germany shifted generally towards the more radical elements in the Nazi party. In November 1937 with the dismissal of Economics Minister Schacht the last obstacle to Goering's ascendancy in the economic field was removed. Whereas Schacht had been acutely conscious of the unfavourable international repercussions 'Aryanisation' was bound to have, Goering, a close friend of Hitler, was contemptuous of foreign opinion and determined to create a 'Jew-free' economy as quickly as possible. In the spring of 1938 Generals Blomberg and Fritsch, opponents of Hitler's forward foreign policy, were removed and Hitler assumed command of the Wehrmacht. The foreign office, too, came under Nazi control when Foreign Minister Neurath was replaced by the ardent Nazi and admirer of Hitler, Joachim von Ribbentrop.

Intensification of the persecution of German Jewry served another function as well: it helped unify a leadership divided by *Reichskristallnacht*. It was not Goering but Goebbels who triggered off the pogrom. In an intrigue typical of life at the top in Nazi Germany he sought to ingratiate himself with Hitler, who was annoyed by the Propaganda Minister's amorous liaisons. When an embassy official in Paris was murdered by a Jewish boy Goebbels played up the anti-Semitic theme in the press and, dashing to Munich where Hitler was taking part in the annual celebration of the 1923 Putsch, secured his consent for 'spontaneous action' on the streets.

'The SA should have a last fling', he is supposed to have exclaimed. But Goering, Himmler and Heydrich, the enemies of Goebbels, were deliberately kept in the dark. Goering at once protested vehemently to Hitler at the wanton damage done by the activists while Himmler and Heydrich deplored the deleterious effect the pogrom was likely to have on their low-key emigration policy. Though Hitler's sympathies lay with the radically-minded Goebbels, he soon fell in with Goering's suggestion that the time had come for a properly co-ordinated and centrally controlled onslaught on Jewish property. In the end the Nazi leaders forgot their differences and co-operated amicably in the intensified persecution of the common enemy. But Goering, not Goebbels, was put in overall charge of the operation which ensured that his industrial friends were the main beneficiaries of Aryanisation and not the small businessmen whom the Nazis were supposed to favour.

As the war clouds gathered ominously in Europe in 1939, Hitler gave vent to his paranoid hatred of Jewry. In January he told an enthusiastic Reichstag that if

International Jewish finance inside and outside of Europe succeeds in involving the nations in another war, the result will not be the bolshevization of the earth and the victory of Judaism but the annihilation of the Jewish race in Europe.

The same month he informed the Czech foreign minister that 'we are going to destroy the Jews. They are not going to get away with what they did on November 9th, 1918' (i.e. when they allegedly 'betrayed' Germany by masterminding the German Revolution). These and other comments in the spring of 1939 are interpreted by 'intentionalist' historians as proof that the physical destruction of Jewry was still Hitler's aim in 1939, as it had been from his first entry into politics in 1919. But it is questionable whether one can assume that because the Holocaust happened every utterance of Hitler's—a man notoriously given to wild talk—must have been leading up to a grand climax in the gas chambers of Auschwitz.

It would seem, on the contrary, as if the Nazis had no very clear idea where they were going in their anti-Semitism, and that Hitler's tendency to side with the big battalions—when they identified themselves—applied in this as in many other areas of State activity. Hence his willingness to support the emigration policy favoured, oddly enough in view of what followed, by the dreaded SS.

As early as 1934 a sub-section of the SS—the SD or Security Department—whilst anxious to reduce Jewish influence in German life, realised the sporadic Brownshirt outbursts against Jews did harm to the German image. Instead they proposed to solve the 'Jewish question' by pursuing an orderly and systematic policy of mass emigration. Since Himmler's star was in the ascendancy in 1936 he sought to extend his empire by acquiring the exclusive right to handle Jewish affairs.

Emigration was not particularly successful. Only 120,000 of Germany's 503,000 Jews had left the country by the end of 1937. Many even returned deluded by the regime's cautious tactics into believing the worst was over. In March 1938 the SS had their big chance when the annexation of Austria added 190,000 Jews to the existing total. This increase appalled anti-Semites anxious to be rid of Jews, not to take in more. Operating from a central office in Vienna Adolf Eichmann of the SD succeeded in forcing 45,000 Jews out of Austria within six months, using confiscated Jewish property to finance their emigration. Goering, who still had overall responsibility for anti-Semitic measures, was greatly impressed by Eichmann's ruthless efficiency. In January 1939 he gave the policy his approval and delegated its execution in Germany to Reinhard Heydrich, chief of the Reich Security Main Office.

In the course of 1939, 78,000 Jews were forced out of Germany and 30,000 out of Bohemia and Moravia. As it was increasingly difficult to find countries willing to receive Jewish refugees, the SD even worked with Zionist organisations to ship as many Jews as possible illegally to Palestine where the British authorities, anxious not to offend Arab susceptibilities, sought to prevent them landing. As emigration to Palestine obviously helped to create the nucleus of a future Jewish State, SS policy was opposed both by the foreign office and by the *Auslands-organisation*, a Nazi agency led by Gauleiter Bohle, both of which favoured dispersal of Jews throughout the world. Hitler, who invariably watched power struggles from the sidelines intervening only rarely and reluctantly did, in fact, support the SS against their rivals.

The outbreak of the war opened up a new and more terrible chapter in the history of the persecution of the Jews. That Hitler was capable of the most cold-blooded crimes was amply demonstrated in September 1939, when he ordered five *Einsatzgruppen*, or action squads, into Poland in the wake of the German armies with instructions to murder tens of thousands of officials, priests and intellectuals in an attempt to deprive the Poles of their ruling class.

While the battles were still raging in Poland the outlines of a new 'solution' of the 'Jewish question' were taking shape.

Hitler informed close associates of plans to remould Eastern Europe on racial lines, turning their peoples into slaves serving a master race of German settlers. As a first step, the three million Polish Jews must be put in ghettos in specified towns in Eastern Poland and finally resettled in a huge reserve south of Lublin. Early in October Himmler was given special powers as Reich commissioner for the strengthening of Germanism in the East, a crucial appointment which placed the Jews completely at the mercy of the SS. Between December 1939 and February 1940, 600,000 Jews from Danzig-West Prussia and the *Wartheland* (the territories annexed to the Reich) were brutally uprooted, forced into cattle trucks and dumped in the *Generalgouvernement* (the remainder of German-occupied Poland governed by Hans Frank). As he already had 1,400,000 Jews under his jurisdiction, he protested to Goering at the strain placed on limited food supplies. The latter, with Hitler's approval, agreed that further transports must have Frank's approval. As this was not forthcoming, Nazi plans came to an abrupt halt. Meanwhile, as it took time to enclose the Jews in ghettos, interim measures forbade them to change residence, subjected them to a curfew, obliged them to wear a yellow star on their clothing and compelled them to perform forced labour for the German conquerors.

Quite why the Lublin resettlement plan was abandoned is unclear. Perhaps the preparations for the Scandinavian and then the Western campaign absorbed Hitler's attention, for it seems unlikely that Frank's intervention was decisive. What is interesting, in view of the belief of 'intentionalist' historians that the Nazis never wavered in their determination to annihilate the Jewish race physically, is the so-called Madagascar Plan. In the summer of 1940, during the closing stages of the French campaign, Nazi leaders seem to have given serious consideration to transporting the four million Jews of Western Europe to this French island, whilst leaving the Eastern Jews in Poland as a deterrent to American intervention in the war.

The Madagascar Plan had been a favourite with anti-Semites in the 1920s. Himmler was immediately enthusiastic. Eichmann, now in the notorious section IV at the Reich Security Main Office, spent many hours in the Tropical Institute in Hamburg studying climatic conditions in Madagascar. With Hitler's approval a plan of action was drafted. During the summer Hitler mentioned Madagascar to several influential figures including Mussolini and Ciano. The plan was killed stone dead by Britain's refusal to capitulate as so confidently expected by the Nazis. As long as Britain controlled the seas, the transportation of Jews to Madagascar was simply impracticable.

There is no doubt that Hitler's decision to attack Russia, finalised in December 1940, had the most profound implications for the future of European Jewry. For Hitler warned his staff that the impending campaign must be fought on racial lines. 'We must depart from the attitude of soldierly comradeship', he told his commanding generals '. . . we are talking about a war of annihilation . . . commissars and members of the GPU (secret police) are criminals and must be dealt with as such . . .' Just before the attack in June 1941 he signed the Commissar Order requiring his generals to have captured commissars shot forthwith. To carry out these instructions four new action squads, composed of SS, criminal police and security police, operated behind the German lines. Although Heydrich's instructions to the higher SS and Police Officers in charge of captured Russian territory only specified 'Jews in the service of party and State', it seems very likely that the action squads were encouraged to execute all the Jews they could lay their hands on—which is exactly what happened. By the winter of 1941/2, 500,000 Jews had already been shot in this first mass extermination of the war. This episode more than anything else probably sealed the fate of European Jewry.

At this point historians differ in their interpretations. Several, including Christopher Browning, Gerald Fleming, Eberhard Jäckel and Andreas Hillgruber, argue that Hitler decided on the Final Solution sometime in the summer of 1941 whilst others, principally Uwe Dietrich Adam, Martin Broszat and Hans Mommsen, maintain that the decision was arrived at only in the late autumn. Behind what may seem a disagreement about a relatively minor matter of timing, lie fundamental differences about Hitler's role in the Third Reich and, specifically, about his role in the genesis of the Holocaust.

The Mommsen–Broszat school occupy a 'structuralist' position, i.e. whilst not disputing that Hitler exerted considerable influence on the course of events, they do not believe he was always the prime mover. The Holocaust, in their view, was not planned by Hitler from the very beginning but developed out of a deteriorating situation not anticipated by the Nazis though probably rendered inevitable by the spiralling radicalism of their visceral anti-Semitism.

On rather thin evidence they argue that the Final Solution was preceded by yet another solution: the resettlement of European Jewry east of the Urals after Russia's defeat, which was confidently expected to be a matter of weeks only. Stiffening Russian resistance wrecked that plan. Yet in October 1941, precisely when it was becoming apparent that the Blitzkrieg had failed, Hitler ordered the transportation of Jews to the eastern territories to begin again. As there was no way out over the Urals and as more and more Jews were forced into the ghettos of Eastern Poland, resources were strained to breaking point and epidemics started to break out. The response of local SS leaders was to begin, on their own initiative, to murder Jews either by shooting or by using mobile gas vans. Sometime in October or November Himmler informed Hitler of this evolving situation and the latter approved the extension of these practices to encompass the whole of European Jewry. It is even conceivable that the initiative was taken not by Hitler but by Himmler.

The explanation offered by Fleming, Jäckel, Hillgruber and others is an 'intentionalist' one, i.e. that Hitler made his decision in the summer of 1941 under no structural pressure but because he believed a Russian collapse imminent and felt that the moment had come to realise a life-long ambition. Whether he gave a specific order to this effect—no written order has ever been found—or more likely supplied 'a prompting initiative' is an open question. At all events, on July 31st Goering ordered Heydrich to complete the task he had given him in January 1939 by 'bringing about a complete solution of the Jewish question within the German sphere of influence in Europe', and requested him to draft a plan to this effect. Significantly enough at the Wannsee Conference, where the details of the Holocaust were worked out, Heydrich referred specifically to this directive as the justification for the meeting.

The evidence, including that of SS men such as Eichmann and Höss, commandant of Auschwitz, suggests that throughout the summer and autumn of 1941 the SS were working feverishly on the new project. Restrictions already placed on Polish Jews were now extended to German Jews. On September 1st all Jews were ordered to wear a yellow star and forbidden to leave their area of residence without permission. In October Himmler completely banned further Jewish emigration. So when Hitler spoke to Himmler in October/November, he merely approved an existing extermination plan. The undeniable chaos in Eastern Poland in the autumn and the localised shootings and gassings came about not because a 'resettlement plan' had been wrecked—the intentionalists deny the existence of such a plan, believing that Hitler kept Goebbels and Rosenberg in the dark and spoke to them of 'resettlement' when he had 'extermination' in mind—but because an impatient Führer ordered deportations from Germany to begin before the extermination installations had been completed.

What is not in doubt is that in January top SS officials met in the Berlin suburb of Wannsee under Heydrich's direction to work out the final details of the Holocaust. Though the participants, characteristically, preferred to avoid the term 'extermination' the intention was clear enough: the Jews were to be worked to death or gassed. Following the conference, work was accelerated on the building of gas chambers and crematoria at several sites in Eastern Poland: Belzec, Sobibor, Treblinka, Majdanek and Auschwitz-Birkenau. For two years the transports continued to roll eastwards from all corners of Europe and the murder squads continued their grisly task until the advancing Russian armies drove the Germans out of Poland. In all, between five and six-and-a-half million Jews perished in one of the most frightful episodes in history.

Finally, we come to the all-important question: how could members of a highly civilised nation like the Germans have committed such horrible crimes? There is no adequate answer. All one can do is point to certain factors in the historical equation. Naturally the Nazis tried to shroud the operation in secrecy by carrying it out in a remote part of Poland. All the same, rumours did circulate about dreadful deeds in the East. No doubt many Germans were pretty indifferent to the fate of the Jews even if they did not believe what they heard. Because of the Nazis' much-publicised resettlement plans, tens of thousands of people were being moved around Europe like pieces on a chessboard, so that some Germans—including those who rounded the Jews up and transported them eastwards—may have suppressed their doubts and tried to believe that the deportations had no sinister implications.

Above all, one must not forget that a dictatorship gradually corrupts the moral fibre of its citizens: to ask too many questions, let alone protest, was to risk arrest and possibly death. But in the twilight atmosphere in the corridors of power where ambitious men were struggling to build up personal empires there were always plenty of willing hands to do the Führer's bidding. In the SS Hitler had a perfect instrument for mass murder.

To what extent the members of the murder squads were sadists, pathological cases, promotion-seekers or automatons with a grossly distorted sense of duty is a complex matter. What is certain is that without these hardened and experienced killers the Holocaust could not have taken place. Finally, Hitler's constant encouragement ensured that the grisly work continued at a time when Germany's military position was deteriorating and it was plainly an act of madness to divert precious resources to mass murder. That the Holocaust did continue is the ultimate proof of the irrationality at the heart of National Socialism.

SOCIAL OUTCASTS IN THE THIRD REICH

Jeremy Noakes

OF all Nazi atrocities, the extermination of the Jews has, rightly, commanded the most attention from historians and the general public. But this understandable preoccupation with the horrors of Nazi anti-Semitism has led people to overlook the fact that the Jews formed only one, albeit the major, target in a broad campaign directed against a variety of groups who were considered to be 'alien to the community' (*gemeinschaftsfremd*), and who often were defined in biological terms. Only recently have historians begun to focus their attention on this hitherto neglected sphere of Nazi policy and action.

Nazism arose in the aftermath of defeat and revolution. In the view of its leaders, and notably of Hitler, the main cause of Germany's collapse had not been military defeat but the disintegration of the home front weakened by years of incompetent leadership, corroded by pernicious ideas of liberal democracy, Marxism and sentimental humanitarianism, and sapped by biological decline which was the result of ignoring the principles of race and eugenics. Their main domestic goal was to create out of the German people, riven by divisions of class, religion and ideology, a new and unified 'national community' (*Volksgemeinschaft*) based on ties of blood and race and infused with a common 'world view'. They believed this united national community would then possess the requisite morale to enable Germany to make a bid for the position as a world power to which she had long aspired. The members of this national community, the 'national comrades' (*Volksgenossen*), were expected to conform to a norm based on certain criteria. A national comrade was expected to be of Aryan race, genetically healthy (*erbgesund*), socially efficient (*leistungsfähig*), and

83

politically and ideologically reliable, which involved not simply passive obedience but active participation in the various organisations of the regime and repeated gestures of loyalty (the Hitler salute, etc.).

On coming to power the Nazis were determined to discriminate against, or persecute, all those who failed to fulfil these criteria and were therefore regarded as being outside the national community. There were three main types of these outsiders which, although they overlap, can be conveniently considered as separate categories. Firstly, ideological enemies—those who propagated or even simply held beliefs and values regarded as a threat to national morale. Secondly, so-called 'asocials'—the socially inefficient and those whose behaviour offended against the social norms of the 'national community'. And thirdly, the biological outsiders—those who were regarded as a threat because of their race or because they were suffering from a hereditary defect. It is with the last two of these categories that this article is concerned.

The third category, that of biological outsiders, consisted of two main groups: those considered undesirable because of their race (the non-Aryans), and those who were unacceptable on eugenic grounds because of hereditary defects which posed a threat to the future of the German race and/or rendered them socially ineffective. Although the racial and eugenic theories which defined these groups were in some respects distinct—not all eugenists were anti-Semitic for example—they shared common origins in biological theories of the late nineteenth century and a common perspective in viewing mankind primarily in biological terms. Individuals were not seen as possessing validity in themselves as human beings and were not judged in terms of their human qualities, but their significance was assessed first and foremost in terms of their physical and mental efficiency as members of a 'race' and they were seen primarily as collections of good or bad genes.

The theory of eugenics—the idea of improving the 'race'

through the encouragement of selective breeding—had become increasingly influential in many countries during the 1920s and 1930s and Germany was no exception. It flourished against a background of concern about declining birthrates and particularly about the destruction of a generation of the healthiest members of the nation in the First World War. There was also growing concern about the impact of modern improvements in welfare, hygiene, and medical care in ensuring the survival of increasing numbers of those with hereditary defects who were thereby allegedly producing a deterioration of the race. Moreover, during this period it was fashionable to attribute many social ills to heredity—habitual criminality, alcoholism, prostitution, and pauperism. Even some on the Left were attracted by eugenics. They tended to make a sharp distinction between the 'genuine' working class and the *Lumpenproletariat*, the 'dregs' of society. Eugenics appeared to offer the prospect of eliminating the *Lumpenproletariat*, traditionally seen since Marx as the tool of reaction.

During the 1920s a number of doctors and psychiatrists in Germany began to propose a policy of sterilisation to prevent those with hereditary defects from procreating. Such a policy of 'negative selection' had already been carried out on a limited scale in the United States where the technique of vasectomy had been developed and was first applied by a prison doctor in 1899. With the economic crisis which began in 1929 such proposals gained increasing support among those involved in the welfare services, since they appeared to offer the prospect not only of substantial savings in the future but also of facilitating the release of some of those in institutional care without fear of their producing defective offspring. Towards the end of 1932 the Prussian authorities prepared a draft law permitting the voluntary sterilisation of those with hereditary defects. Those who drafted the law had felt obliged to make sterilisation voluntary since they believed that public opinion was not yet ready for compulsion. The logic of the eugenist case, however, required compulsion and, significantly, the Nazi medical experts who took part in the preceding discussions had demanded compulsion. The sterilisation issue was given priority by Hitler himself who overruled objections from his Catholic Vice-Chancellor, von Papen. On July 14th, 1933, within six months of its coming to power, the new regime had issued a Sterilisation Law ordering the sterilisation—by compulsion if necessary—of all those suffering from a number of specified illnesses which were alleged to be hereditary.

Apart from the moral issues raised by the question of compulsory sterilisation as such, the criteria used to define hereditary illness were in many respects exceedingly dubious. Thus, while there could be no doubt about the hereditary nature of some of the diseases specified, such as Huntingdon's Chorea, others such as 'hereditary simple-mindedness', schizophrenia, manic depressive illness, and 'chronic alcoholism' were not only more difficult to diagnose but their hereditary basis was much more questionable. Moreover, even if it were granted, the elimination of these diseases through the sterilisation of those affected was an impossible task in view of the role played by recessive genes in their transmission. Finally, although an impressive apparatus of hereditary courts was established to pass judgment on the individual cases, the evidence used to justify proposals for sterilisation sometimes reflected more the social and political prejudices of the medical and welfare authorities involved than objective scientific criteria. Thus a reputation for being 'work-shy' or even former membership of the Communist Party could be used as crucial supporting evidence in favour of sterilisation. From 1934 to 1945 between 320,000 and 350,000 men and women were sterilised under this law and almost one hundred people died following the operation. After the war few of those sterilised received any compensation for what they had suffered since they could not claim to have been persecuted on political or racial grounds. The new measure appears to have had at least tacit support from public opinion. It was only when people found members of their own families, friends and colleagues affected by it that they became concerned.

The Nazis claimed that sterilisation was an unfortunate necessity for those with hereditary defects and that once it was carried out the sterilised were thereby in effect restored to full status as 'national comrades'. In practice, however, in a society in which health, and in particular fertility, were key virtues the sterilised were bound to feel discriminated against, and the fact that they were forbidden to marry fertile partners underlined this point. However, for those who were not merely suffering from hereditary defects but were socially ineffective as well the future was far bleaker. Already in 1920 a distinguished jurist, Karl Binding, and a psychiatrist, Alfred Hoche, had together published a book with the title: *The Granting of Permission for the Destruction of Worthless Life. Its Extent and Form.* In this book, written under the impression of the casualties of the First World War, the two authors proposed that in certain cases it should be legally possible to kill those suffering from incurable and severely crippling handicaps and injuries—so-called 'burdens on the community' (*Ballastexistenzen*). This proposal assumed, first, that it was acceptable for an outside agency to define what individual life was 'worthless' and, secondly, that in effect an individual had to justify his existence according to criteria imposed from outside (i.e. he had to prove that his life was worthwhile). These assumptions were indeed implicit in the biological and collectivist approach to human life which had become increasingly influential after 1900.

With the take-over of power by the Nazis it was not long before this biological and collectivist approach began to be transferred from theory into reality. In addition to the sterilisation programme, this took the form, firstly, of a propaganda campaign designed to devalue the handicapped as burdens on the community in the eyes of the population and, secondly, of a programme of systematic extermination of the mentally sick and handicapped—the so-called Euthanasia Programme, a misleading title since the term 'euthanasia' was in fact a Nazi euphemism for mass murder.

The euthanasia programme began in the spring or early summer of 1939 when the parents of a severely handicapped baby petitioned Hitler for the baby to be killed. He agreed to the request and ordered the head of his personal Chancellery, Phillip Bouhler, to proceed likewise in all similar cases. Bouhler set up a secret organisation to carry out the programme which initially covered children up to three years old, later extended to sixteen years. By the end of the war approximately 5,000 children had been murdered either by injection or through deliberate malnutrition. In August 1939 Hitler ordered that the extermination programme be extended to adults, for which the Führer's Chancellery set up another secret organisation. So large were the numbers involved—there were approximately 200,000 mentally sick and handicapped in 1939 —that a new method of killing had to be devised. Experts in the Criminal Police Department came up with the idea of using carbon monoxide gas. After a successful trial on a few patients, gas chambers were constructed in six mental hospitals in various parts of Germany to which patients were transferred from mental institutions all over the Reich. By the time the programme was officially stopped by Hitler in August 1941 under pressure from public protests some 72,000 people had been murdered.

During the next two years under a separate programme also run by the Führer's Chancellery under the code number 14F13, the reference number of the Inspector of Concentration Camps, another 30–50,000 people were selected from concentration camps and gassed on the grounds of mental illness, physical incapacity, or simply racial origin, in which case the 'diagnosis' on the official form read 'Jew' or 'gypsy'. In the meantime, however, the majority of the personnel who had developed expertise in operating the gas chambers had been transferred to Poland and placed at the disposal of the SS for the death camps which opened in the winter of 1941/2. These notorious death camps—Belzec, Treblinka, Sobibor, Majdanek, and Auschwitz-Birkenau—were intended to destroy the other biological outcasts of Nazi Germany, the non-Aryans, of whom the Jews formed by far the largest group. However, the understandable preoccupation with the Holocaust has tended to divert attention from another group which came into this category—the gypsies. For they also suffered genocide at the hands of the Nazis.

Long before the Nazis came to power the gypsies had been treated as social outcasts. Their foreign appearance, their strange customs and language, their nomadic way of life and lack of regular employment had increasingly come to be regarded as an affront to the norms of a modern State and society. They were seen as asocial, a source of crime, culturally inferior, a foreign body within the nation. During the 1920s, the police, first in Bavaria and then in Prussia, established special offices to keep the gypsies under constant surveillance. They were photographed and fingerprinted as if they were criminals. With the Nazi take-over, however, a new motive was added to the grounds for persecution—their distinct and allegedly inferior racial character.

Nazi policy towards the gypsies, like the policy towards the Jews, was uncertain and confused. Initially they were not a major target. With their small numbers—30,000—and generally low social status they were not seen as such a serious racial threat as the Jews. They were, however, included in the regulations implementing the Nürnberg Law for the Protection of German Blood and Honour of September 15th, 1935, which banned marriage and sexual relations between Aryans and non-Aryans. From then onwards they were the subject of intensive research by racial 'experts' of the 'Research Centre for Racial Hygiene and Biological Population Studies'. The aim was to identify and distinguish between pure gypsies and the part-gypsies (*Mischlinge*) who had been lumped together in the records of the Weimar police. Whereas in the case of the Jews the *Mischlinge* were treated as less of a threat than the 'full' Jews, among the gypsies the *Mischlinge*, some of whom had integrated themselves into German society, were treated as the greater threat. The leading expert on the gypsies, Dr Robert Ritter, insisted that:

The gypsy question can only be regarded as solved when the majority of a-social and useless gypsy *Mischlinge* have been brought together in large camps and made to work and when the continual procreation of this half-breed population has been finally prevented. Only then will future generations be freed from this burden.

In December 1938 Himmler issued a 'Decree for the Struggle against the Gypsy Plague', which introduced a more systematic registration of gypsies based on the research of the racial experts. Pure gypsies received brown papers, gypsy *Mischlinge* light blue ones and nomadic non-gypsies grey ones. The aim was 'once and for all to ensure the racial separation of gypsies from our own people to prevent the mixing of the two races, and finally to regulate the living conditions of the gypsies and gypsy *Mischlinge*'. After the victory over Poland the deportation of gypsies from Germany to Poland was ordered, and in the meantime they were forbidden to leave the camps to which they were assigned and which were now in effect turned into labour camps. In May 1940 2,800 gypsies joined the Jewish transports to Poland. However, this deportation programme was then stopped because of logistical problems in the reception areas.

During 1941–2 gypsies and gypsy *Mischlinge* were included in the discriminatory measures introduced against Jews within the Reich and they were also removed from the Armed Forces. However, while there was unanimous contempt for the gypsy *Mischlinge*, Nazi racial experts had a certain admiration for the way in which the pure gypsies had sustained their separate identity and way of life over the centuries, an achievement attributed to their strong sense of race. Dr Robert Ritter suggested that the 'pure bred' gypsies in Germany (*Sinti*) and in the German-speaking areas of Bohemia and Moravia (*Lalleri*) should be assigned to an area where they would be permitted to live according to their traditional ways more or less as museum specimens, while the remainder should be sterilised, interned, and subjected to forced labour. Himmler sympathised with this view and in October 1942 issued orders for appropriate arrangements to be made. However, he ran into opposition from Bormann and probably Hitler and so, on December 16th, 1942, he issued an order for the German gypsies to be transferred to Auschwitz. Between February 26th and March 25th, 1943, 11,400 gypsies from Germany and elsewhere were transported to a special gypsy camp within Auschwitz. Here, unlike other prisoners, they were able to live together with their families, probably to facilitate the medical experiments which were carried out in a medical centre established in their camp by the notorious Dr Mengele. Of the 20,000 gypsies in all transported to Auschwitz, 11,000 were murdered there, while the others were transferred elsewhere. At the same time, thousands of gypsies were being murdered throughout occupied Europe, notably by the *Einsatzgruppen* in Russia. It has been estimated that half a million European gypsies died at the hands of the Nazis. Of the 30,000 gypsies living in Germany in 1939 only 5,000 survived the war.

The gypsies offended against the norms of the 'national community' not only on the grounds of their non-Aryan character (although ironically since they had originated in India they could legitimately claim to be more 'Aryan' than the Germans!), but also on the grounds of their 'asocial' behaviour. The 'asocials' formed another major category of social outcasts. The term 'asocial' was a very flexible one which could be used to include all those who failed to abide by the social norms of the national community: habitual criminals, the so-called 'work-shy', tramps and beggars, alcoholics, prostitutes, homosexuals, and juvenile delinquents. The Nazis introduced much tougher policies towards such groups, in some cases—as with the Sterilisation Law—implementing measures which had been demanded or planned before their take-over of power. Above all, there was a growing tendency for the police to acquire more and more control over these groups at the expense of the welfare agencies and the courts. It was the ultimate ambition of the police to take over responsibility for all those whom it defined as 'community aliens' (*Gemeinschaftsfremde*). To achieve this goal, in 1940 it introduced a draft 'Community Alien Law' which, after being held up by opposition from other government departments, was finally intended to go into effect in 1945. According to Paragraph 1.i of the final draft:

A person is alien to the community if he/she proves to be incapable of satisfying the minimum requirements of the national community through his/her own efforts, in particular through an unusual degree of deficiency of mind or character.

The official explanation of the law maintained that:

The National Socialist view of welfare is that it can only be granted to national comrades who both need it and are worthy of it. In the case of community aliens who are only a burden on the national community welfare is not necessary, rather police compulsion with the aim of either making them once more useful members of the national community through appropriate measures or of preventing them from being a further burden. In all these matters protection of the community is the primary object.

In September 1933, the Reich Ministries of the Interior and Propaganda initiated a major round-up of 'tramps and beggars' of whom there were between 300,000 and 500,000, many of them homeless young unemployed. Such a large number of people without fixed abode was regarded as a threat to public order. However, the regime lacked the means to provide shelter and work for such vast numbers. Moreover, there were advantages in having a mobile labour force which could if necessary be directed to particular projects. The Nazis, therefore, initially made a distinction between 'orderly' and 'disorderly' people of no fixed abode. Those who were healthy, willing to work, and with no previous convictions were given a permit (*Wanderkarte*) and were obliged to follow particular routes and perform compulsory work in return for their board and lodging. 'Disorderly' persons of no fixed abode on the other hand could be dealt with under the Law against Dangerous Habitual Criminals and concerning Measures for Security and Correction of November 24th, 1933, and the Preventive Detention Decree of the Ministry of the Interior of December 14th, 1937, which introduced the practice of preventive detention. Many tramps were also sterilised.

After 1936, as a result of the economic recovery, Germany faced a growing labour shortage and the regime was no longer willing to tolerate either numbers of people of no fixed abode or the 'work-shy'. Apart from their significance for the labour force, such people contradicted basic principles of the national community—the principle of performance and the principle of being 'integrated' (*erfassteingeordnet*). As one Nazi expert put it:

In the case of a long period without work on the open road where he is entirely free to follow his own desires and instincts, he (the tramp) is in danger of becoming a freedom fanatic who rejects all integration as hated compulsion.

As a result, persons of no fixed abode increasingly came to be regarded as a police rather than a welfare matter. Even before 1936 some people designated as 'work-shy' had been sent to concentration camps forming the category of 'asocials' who wore a black triangle. A big round-up had taken place before the Olympic games and in 1936 two of the ten companies in Dachau were composed of this category. In the summer of 1938 an even bigger round-up took place under the code word 'Work-shy Reich' in the course of which approximately 11,000 'beggars, tramps, pimps and gypsies' were arrested and transferred largely to Buchenwald where they formed the largest category of prisoner until the influx of Jews following the 'Night of Broken Glass' on November 8th. It has been estimated that some 10,000 tramps were incarcerated in concentration camps during the Third Reich of whom few survived the ordeal. This harsh policy towards the 'asocials' appears to have been popular with many Germans and was welcomed by local authorities who were thereby able to get rid of their 'awkward customers'.

Having set up a utopian model of an ideologically and racially homogeneous 'national community', the Nazis increasingly sought an explanation for deviance from its norms not in terms of flaws within the system itself and its incompatibility with human variety but rather in terms of flaws which were innate within the individual. As an anti-type to the racially pure, genetically healthy, loyal and efficient 'national comrade', they evolved the concept of the 'degenerate asocial' whose deviance was *biologically* determined. As the Reich Law Leader, Hans Frank, put it in a speech in October 1938:

National Socialism regards degeneracy as an immensely important source of criminal activity. It is our belief that every superior nation is furnished with such an abundance of endowments for its journey through life that the word 'degeneracy' most clearly defines the state of affairs that concerns us here. In a decent nation the 'genus' must be regarded as valuable *per se*: consequently, in an individual degeneracy signifies exclusion from the normal *genus* of the decent nation. This state of being degenerate, this different or alien quality tends to be rooted in miscegenation between a decent representative of his race and an individual of inferior stock. To us National Socialists criminal biology, or the theory of congenital criminality, connotes a link between racial decadence and criminal manifestations. The complete degenerate lacks all racial sensitivity and sees it as his positive duty to harm the community or member thereof. He is the absolute opposite of the man who recognises that the fulfilment of his duty as a national comrade is his mission in life.

These ideas represent a variation on concepts which had emerged from research into so-called 'criminal biology' which had been going on in the Weimar Republic. Nor was this simply a matter of theory. For the Nazis had actually begun to apply the principles of criminal biology in the sphere of juvenile delinquency. This was another area in which the police usurped the responsibility of the welfare agencies and the courts. In 1939 they exploited the Preventive Detention Decree of 1937 to set up their own Reich Central Agency for the Struggle against Juvenile Delinquency and the following year established a Youth Concentration Camp in Moringen near Hannover. Perhaps the most significant feature of the camp was the fact that the youths were subjected to 'biological and racial examination' under the supervision of Dr Ritter, now the Director of the Criminal-Biological Institute of the Reich Security Main Office. Then, on the basis of highly dubious pseudo-scientific criteria, they were divided into groups according to their alleged socio-biological character and reformability. This process of socio-biological selection pioneered in Moringen was an integral part of the concept of the Community Aliens Law. Thus, according to the official justification of the Law:

The governments of the period of the System (Weimar) failed in their measures to deal with community aliens. They did not utilise the findings of genetics and criminal biology as a basis for a sound welfare and penal policy. As a result of their liberal attitude they constantly perceived only the 'rights of the individual' and were more concerned with his protection from state intervention than with the general good. In National Socialism the individual counts for nothing when the community is at stake.

Defeat preserved Germans from being subjected to the Community Aliens Law and a future in which any deviation from the norms of the 'national community' would be not merely criminalised but also liable to be defined as evidence of 'degeneracy', i.e. biological inadequacy, for which the penalties were sterilisation and probably eventual 'eradication' (*Aus-merzen*) through hard labour in concentration camp conditions. The Third Reich's policy towards social outcasts stands as a frightful warning both against the application of pseudo-science to social problems and against the rationalisation of social prejudices in terms of pseudo-science.

GOOD TIMES, BAD TIMES:
MEMORIES OF THE
THIRD REICH

Ulrich Herbert

As late as 1951 almost half of those citizens of the Federal Republic of Germany questioned in a public opinion survey described the period between 1933 and 1939 as the one in which things had gone best for Germany.

All 'politics' aside, for a large part of the population the image of National Socialism was characterised principally not by terror, mass murder and war but by reduction of unemployment, economic boom, tranquillity and order. In 1949 the *Institut für Demoskopie* (Public Opinion Institute) summarised the result of its survey of the 'Consequences of National Socialism'. There was 'no more talk of German rebirth or of racial awakening among the population; these bits of Third Reich décor are antiquated, worn out, finished'. On the other hand, memories of the 'positive' aspects of National Socialism were still as fresh as ever:

The guaranteed pay packet, order, *KdF* [Kraft durch Freude, Strength through Joy, the National Socialist leisure organisation] and the smooth running of the political machinery . . . Thus 'National Socialism' makes them think merely of work, adequate nourishment, *KdF* and the absence of 'disarray' in political life.

The result of these post-war opinion surveys into the German people's memories of Nazism correspond at many points to the findings of a large oral-history project that has been carried out for the past four years at the universities of Essen and Hagen under the direction of Lutz Niethammer: *Life History and Social Culture in the Ruhr, 1930–1960*. The source material for the part of the project discussed here consisted of the narrated life histories of elderly blue-collar and white-collar workers from Essen, most of whom had worked for many years in the Krupp steel works and who were aged between sixty-five and seventy-five at the time of the interviews. Today they are almost all Social Democrats in their political sympathies; in the 1920s and 1930s they belonged to the socialist workers' movement. None of them was a National Socialist.

I shall reproduce here, in condensed form, some of the conclusions and reflections that have arisen from this project. By way of illustration I shall begin by presenting a shortened version of one of the narrated life histories—one that is in many ways typical of the bulk of the 200 or so interviews that have been conducted and analysed in the course of the research.

Ernst Bromberg, born 1905, fitter: Herr Bromberg is today well over seventy. For fifteen years he has been a pensioner. He sings regularly in a Protestant church choir, has voted SPD ever since the war and was a trade-union shop steward for many years. His father worked for Krupp, and thus there was no question but that he would as well. He began working for Krupp on April 8th, 1920, first as an errand boy, then as an apprentice. He still vividly recalls his work in the 1920s. He describes precisely and down to the smallest detail not only his own job but also each individual working procedure, the machines, the products and the different stages of the production process. This period, he frequently emphasises, was a particularly hard one: his father died young, he had to support his mother out of his meagre wages. Between 1927 and 1932 he was dismissed five times 'owing to lack of work'.

The account of his life story up to 1932 is marked by alternations of employment and unemployment and the persistent uncertainty of the situation in both a social and a political sense. His only positive memories from this period are of the free time spent with his Protestant youth group and with the church choir. In 1932 he finally got another job with Krupp, which he then kept for a long period—and with the year 1932 his hitherto unbroken narrative flow also begins to falter:

Well, then I gradually got fed up—so I got married. That was '32. Oh God, the things that happened then—the years went by, the children were born, '33, '36, '39, the war came, I moved to the *Heimaterde* [Home Soil] housing estate up in Mülheim, in '43 I was transferred, because they'd smashed our works to bits—the machines were packed away, the tools packed away, what was left of them, and then every day so-and-so many people were put on the train and off they went to Mülhausen.

The reference to the evacuation of the plant marks the beginning of a new section of his narrative, which he again reports in detail and in chronological sequence; he has nothing else specific to say about the time between 1932 and 1943.

The National Socialist period itself is characterised in his memory by work, family life and free time spent with colleagues from the Protestant church choir; he had scarcely anything to do with the 'whole political business':

No time for it, when you're on three-shift working—with the Labour Front, later on—oh God, yes—people kicked against it a bit and then it just carried on, you know! Yes, well obviously, if you were on piece work, you didn't have any time to make speeches, you got up in the morning when you had to, you didn't overstretch your break periods —because after all—the money was tempting . . . I didn't worry any more about the Nazis, put it that way, apart from my Labour Front contribution I just didn't have anything to do with the Nazis, you know—and anyway I was tied up with my Protestant clubs all week, you know . . . Nothing really changed there.

Herr Bromberg stressed that this was also a period of economic advancement for him. He never produced substandard work; he always earned the highest piece rate in his section, and he never slacked off. He continued to meet his colleagues in his church group and the brass band, even though this became steadily more difficult. Because of the triple shift system and his family duties, he could not take part in rehearsals so regularly. For the rest, time went by, 'quietly and without much song and dance'.

With the evacuation of the works in 1943, his account becomes more lively again. He describes the individual stages of the evacuation of the works: Mülhausen, Kulmbach, Nürnberg. He describes the bombing raids, the laborious attempts to get production going again, his brief induction into the *Volkssturm* [home guard] ('Bang, bang, that was the end of the *Volkssturm*') and coming under fire from dive bombers— 'and one day the Yanks came, and the war was over'.

He scraped his way back to Essen, couldn't find work there, eventually went to his family in Thuringia, where they had been evacuated. There he found a job in a metal works, and a flat. When describing this period he stresses particularly the problems of obtaining supplies and political difficulties with his foreman, and also his son's progress in school. In 1954 the family returned to Essen. After a short spell with another firm he joined Krupp again, in his old factory. The 'unprompted' part of his narrative ends when he obtains a flat in Essen in 1955, though he immediately adds a reference to his retirement in 1967; he skips over the twelve years in between. When asked, he says that he did only individual piece-work right through until 1967, spent his free time going to the choral society, didn't earn bad money, later became shop steward—but none of this is described in more detail; it is merely mentioned. 'Everyone knows what it's like.'

Two phases of disturbed and socially insecure existence characterise Herr Bromberg's story: the phase up to 1932, until life moves on to a more even keel thanks to marriage and a safe job; and that between 1943 and 1954. About the phases he calls the 'quiet times'—1932–43, and from 1954 onwards—he volunteers little, and when questioned has no more to add: work, family, and a little free time, and that was it.

As with Ernst Bromberg, so with most of the other elderly

interviewees: it is the breaks in the accounts of their own life stories that stand out. Without exception these breaks are marked by personal turning points in their lives rather than by political events. Whereas the period up to the ending of insecurity and frequent unemployment in the mid-1930s is described at length and in detail, the narrators have little to report about the next phase, until they are directly affected by the war through military conscription or Allied bombing raids on their home town. The third phase, however, from the individual's entry into the war until roughly the currency reform of 1948, is again described precisely and in full. The period from the beginning of the 1950s again throws up few memories that seem worth recording. 'Quiet', 'normal' times, then, clearly leave behind few experiences that are imprinted on the memory and recalled in the narratives; 'disturbed', 'bad' times are filled with unique and extraordinary experiences, and come up at corresponding length in the life stories.

The only remarkable thing about this would seem to be that the years between 1935 and 1942 appear as 'quiet' and 'normal' times—and this in the recollections of inhabitants of a working-class region where in the first years of dictatorship the labour movement suffered the fiercest persecution.

Let us therefore examine the separate narrative phases more closely, in order to get a more precise view of the way in which the Nazi period has been treated in these life stories.

In the accounts of the first phase three elements predominate:
—*Childhood in the working-class family:* the parents are poor, have to work hard and are closely tied into a specific cultural and/or political context: the Protestant congregation, the labour movement, or neighbours in the works housing estate.
—*Leisure time in the youth group:* 'happy memories' of fellowship in Protestant youth groups, of workers' sport organisations or trade-union youth activity are consistently depicted as shaping the whole of subsequent personal development.
—*The social and political unrest of the early 1930s:* here the

precise descriptions of the constant shifting between employment and unemployment or short-time working are particularly striking.

The fact that the period of youth is recalled and described in intense detail is not surprising. But there is a particular wealth of temporal reference-points here, marking off separate stages of life. Social hardship, especially, is a sort of leitmotif in this first phase, both as experienced within the family and in general. What is striking is that, on the one hand, the descriptions of hardship, the often oppressive overcrowding at home, insecurity and instability run side by side with thoroughly positive memories of 'intact family life' and happy, fulfilled time spent with other young people; and, on the other, that there is a pre-echo in the narratives of the fact that things did not continue in this way. This phase of life—irrespective of how long it lasted in individual cases—is depicted as a condition that certainly arouses good memories but that ultimately could not be sustained and had to be altered. For most of those affected this phase extended beyond the usual age: as against the experience of unrest, uncertainty and instability, especially in the world of work, the stability of the youth groups and circles of friends persisted, mainly within the social milieu inherited from the parents. The more unstable the individual's own situation, the stronger the ties to the social milieu; yet in the accounts these same ties are presented as expedients.

Then very abruptly, often datable to the precise day, a quite different focus appears in the life stories: there is always a break in the narrative when the individual gets the job that he then keeps for many years thereafter. And it seems that this turning-point was also perceived as such at the time. The time-budget was completely transformed: time that previously was so abundant suddenly became scarce; the secure job often brought marriage and family in its train. In all the reports the men speak from this point on only of their individual development. The group, previously so dominant in the narratives, falls into the background. Instead of 'we' they speak of 'I'; the unbroken chronological narrative ceases. When questioned, they offer greater detail about the realms of 'work', 'family' and 'leisure', as well as about their attitudes towards the National Socialists, but these subjects are not treated as integrated components of a life history, as realms of experience which are distinct and separated one from the other.

Work and family appear as interdependent: the secure job finally makes it possible to start a family; the need to support the family justifies the job and the acceptance of overtime and piece-work. The two are portrayed jointly as finally allowing an end to the protracted phase of adolescence that had been brought about by adverse circumstances. Circumstances become 'normal', it is commonly said. It is interesting what happens to the bonds with the previously so important youth peer-group. Where the stability of the links with the social environment previously had been a function of the instability of circumstances, this relation was now inverted. Secondary stabilisation via the milieu had lost its function; it was superseded by a new perspective directed towards individual advancement.

For a considerable portion of the male population of the Ruhr this phase of peaceful development lasted longer than it did elsewhere. 1939 meant the start of active participation in the war for relatively few of these men, since the armaments industry naturally had a high quota of workers in reserved occupations. It was not until the end of 1942, when the massive employment of foreign workers and prisoners of war really made itself felt, that even in the Ruhr the proportion of men being conscripted rose.

The core of this peaceful phase was a new long-term perspective comprising secure employment, the starting and bringing up of a family, and increasingly looser ties with old friends and colleagues. These ties gradually took on a new function: they no longer served as a stabiliser, since the individual's existence itself had now stabilised, but acted increasingly as a shield against the outside. Within this narrower context, as one man says, 'politics didn't matter'; everyone's behaviour was such that 'we all still got on well together after the war'; Nazi attempts to organise people were fended off; 'politics' was not allowed to disturb the rhythm of life.

The main focus in the private sphere, however, was clearly the family; the close connection between family and social environment was destroyed. Life in the workplace, life within the family, and life in a social context that now became a 'circle of acquaintances' are now portrayed as separate spheres of experience, connected only through the person of the narrator. Here may lie one of the reasons for the break in the narrative flow: life was now running in orderly fashion, but its separate spheres were fragmented and did not produce a meaningful interconnected whole such as might be presented in a life story.

When the individual gets directly involved in the events of the war the narrative style changes. Life becomes structured by definite reference-points, and its rhythm dominated by the incursion of external events that affect aspects of life. For example, the account of one Krupp employee born in 1909 is structured around the air raids on Essen, a short spell in the military at the end of the war, and time spent cleaning up rubble; his own work, family life, and activities in the Krupp housing estate on the edge of Essen are mentioned only as these war-related events encroach upon them. Ernst Bromberg describes the to-and-fro caused by the destruction of the factory, evacuation, further destruction, transfer, destruction, further transfer. For this period he no longer relates memories of a private life in the narrower sense. Although in retrospect the National Socialist State's provision of a quiet and secure life is evaluated very positively in principle, the experiences during the war gave the lie to the pretences of Nazism: the self-propelling dynamics of Nazi politics, which during the previous years always had been left 'outside', now destroyed that private domain that had only just been built up (without the individual himself feeling that he had contributed to the destruction in any way himself).

The long wartime and post-war phase is portrayed as one of intense experiences in two respects: as a time of suffering, and as a significant time for extending one's capabilities. It is seen as a time of suffering in that the 'normality' attained with such difficulty was destroyed and seemed unlikely to be reconstructed for a long time. After the evacuation of one's factory, the destruction of one's home or the beginning of military service, neither regular work nor a family life appeared likely in the near future. In this situation the individual fought his own way through adversity; the sharper you were, the better your chance of success. With this went the other aspect of how this period was experienced: descriptions of life in the army, in the Labour Service or in the factory also involve accounts of individuals scaling barriers that previously had been regarded as insurmountable. Thus Ernst Bromberg and others suddenly have to train whole groups of Soviet 'Eastern workers'; others rise to become non-commissioned officers and suddenly have to take on administrative tasks far more demanding than those they previously knew in the factory or at the office.

Re-entry into 'normal life' marks the third narrative turning-point. It occurs whenever the separate spheres of private life have been rebuilt: a secure job, an intact flat, and the sense that long-term plans can be made once again. Reconstruction—and that means the reconstruction of the conditions of the 1930s—can begin.

This very reference to the experiences of 'normal life' seems particularly problematic. In the recollections of the 1930s individual, private circumstances and 'politics' appear completely unrelated to one another. This can be observed clearly with regard to the area of work. Work is portrayed as the absolutely central experience in this phase, laying claim to the entire time-budget and virtually cutting the individual off from the outside world. Individual performance at work is emphasised more heavily than anything else. The worker's experiences in his own factory, or at least in the more immediate surroundings of his section or workshop, are entirely positive, that is first and foremost free of politics. The dominance of the sphere of work over all others is described as a qualitatively new experience. The fresh memory of personal and general unemployment meant that the curtailment and final destruction of the social achievements of the Weimar period was regarded as less important than the advantage of having a secure job. The important things were the individual's own performance at work and his skill.

The pride in work that clearly emerges is not a product of the experience of Nazism, however. It arises from the tradition of an ideology of work that was characteristic of the history of organised labour long before National Socialism. The 'good work' that the individual delivers can also be interpreted as a moral symbol, representing the worker's identity and self-confidence, in reaction to the increasing rationalisation of the labour process.

Herr Bromberg's statement that he never produced substandard work exemplifies his and others' valuation of work as an end in itself, as a matter of pride, and as a means for the assertion of self-esteem. This work ethic is by no means the monopoly of apolitical or Social Democratic interviewees—as is shown by the case of Herr Terjung, who as a Communist had considerable political difficulties in his factory and in 1943 was finally ordered off to the Eastern Front as punishment. He describes his work experiences thus:

Then I was chosen because of my special qualifications and I went—I was transferred prematurely to a firm, a firm engaged in precision work . . . An old foreman came and stood by my bench and watched my work for a good half hour, and he said to me 'Herr Terjung,' he said, 'you're going straight on to piece-work, you know how to work all right! And,' he said, 'I don't agree that you should be cheated of your rightful earnings.'

This quotation contains almost everything: the special qualifications, which set one apart from others; the work in a precision firm, where what counts is not physical strength but skill; the old, experienced superior; the just wage, determined by the individual's capabilities; and finally the tone in which the foreman addresses him: 'Herr Terjung'—a good worker is addressed as '*Sie*' (the polite form of 'you').

The factory is seen as a self-contained universe in which the individual's qualifications lead to just rewards, protection against the Nazis and the preservation of dignity. However, the fact that dissent from Nazi politics was manifested by barring Nazis from the inner realms of the world of work—that 'one didn't want to have anything to do with the Nazis'—does not mean that there were no positive reactions to what the National Socialist State had to offer.

This is particularly true of leisure. The men's accounts of their youth in the Weimar period repeatedly refer to the 'pleasant trips' they made. Walking tours through the Münsterland with Protestant youth groups, or weekend excursions nearer home with workers' sports clubs, evoke positive memories, but at the same time they are always the product of the plentiful 'spare time' that resulted from unemployment or short-time working. Leisure time in the 1930s is described quite differently. Journeys into the surrounding countryside now frequently take place with the family, and new leisure activities become available. 'I've never been to the theatre as much as I did then,' says one, and in all the interviews the 'Strength through Joy' tours crop up as 'a really good thing'. Holiday journeys to distant places in Germany or even abroad represent especially clearly the separation of family leisure from the social milieu; the cycling tour with the youth group now gives way to the holiday with a big anonymous organisation. Leisure takes on an active role, and no longer functions as a stopgap, filling up superfluous 'free' time created by unemployment. The 'pleasant trip' becomes the 'marvellous holiday'; enforced idleness is replaced by 'the most precious weeks of the year'.

Even opponents of the Nazis can look back quite positively on the 'Strength through Joy' journeys. The basis for this is the splitting of life into distinct, separate realms. Partial dissent *vis-à-vis* Nazi policies is quite compatible with consent in other areas. It is thus quite possible even for political opponents of the Nazi regime to describe the pre-war years as 'quiet' or 'normal' times. This stress on normality is also a reaction to what are assumed to be the expectations of the interviewer. But the central point is that the period can be described as one of peaceful private advance because 'politics' has been banished to areas beyond the individual awareness—in order to live as well as to survive.

It is natural to ask whether more can be made of the conspicuous silence about both the 1930s and the 1950s than merely to establish the parallels between the periods. The fact that many aspects of pre-1945 tradition were taken up again from the 1950s onwards has been depicted by critics of the Federal Republic virtually as a congenital defect that hindered a genuinely fresh political start. The question is whether connections can be traced between the 1930s and 1950s which go beyond political traditions to point to an explanation of the massive (if not rapturous) approval accorded the new republic in the course of the 1950s.

In the interviews the later post-war period is described as the phase in which one attempted to make a fresh start. The phase ends at the moment when the narrative reaches this new starting-point. The question of what was learned from what had gone before and how that experience was applied in the fresh start of the 1950s does not arise explicitly; it receives an implicit answer all the same.

The old social milieu is never mentioned in this new context. It is tied up with memories of youth, and in any case these ties had largely been destroyed by the trend towards individualism and the Nazi terror of the 1930s, as well as by the destruction of working-class districts in wartime air raids; the imperialism of the National Socialists had been discredited by defeat, and once the war is over, value-based non-materialist perspectives ceased to exist. The preparations for, and establishment of, the Federal Republic itself, the new democratic beginning, is thus scarcely remembered as such but only as 'a lot of speech-making'; the process seems to have passed large sections of the population by. Only the currency reform, the start of economic recovery directed from above, is mentioned—quite the opposite of an ideological perspective.

Of all that the interviewees have experienced up to this point, only the pre-war period evokes positive memories. The interviews leave little doubt that 'reconstruction' meant essentially picking up from where these 1930s experiences left off: secure employment, well-ordered family life, and politics kept at arms' length.

The general silence about these phases and the characterisation of both as 'normal times' can perhaps be explained through the experience of long-term socio-economic stability that began in the 1950s. For these men this phase is still not at an end; it has gone on for thirty years without a break, and no real historical relationship to it exists. This period has shaped the definition of normal life: this *is* normality. No act of memory is needed in order to demonstrate what this period was—or rather, is—like. It is seen as contemporary. Only what is seen as history—previous history—is remembered and can be related; it is distinguished precisely by having been different from the way things are now. With this in mind, one might ask whether the 1930s, too, are perceived as the 'normal condition': as a trial run for the present, so to speak, providing the model for the reconstruction of the 1950s.

Yet the interviews also show that the 1940s are perhaps more than just an irksome interruption of the continuity between 1935 and the present. The increase in qualifications and mobility which most of the interviewees had during the war and the post-war period not only shattered the old social environment for good; it also aroused hopes of improvement among manual workers and lower-level white-collar workers which continued to be felt in the 1950s and which found their latest fulfilment through the school-leaving certificates of the men's children. The emphasis on the 'good worker's' individual work capabilities also has undergone a change in function. Whereas in the 1930s it served as a bulwark only against Nazi attempts to organise people at the workplace, it now functions as a barrier against politics generally. But these changes between the 1930s and 1950s are not made explicit in the interviews. Memories of the 'bad times' of the 1940s have scarcely been integrated in the life histories; they seem to be nothing more than one single long traumatic experience that serves as the negative counterpart to (and almost defines) the 'good times' that preceded and followed them.

Thus in retrospect the 1930s and 1950s both seem 'quiet', 'good', times, and the period of the 'first economic miracle' under the Nazis appears as a sort of precursor to the 1950s. After the forced interruption of total war and the immediate post-war years, the 1950s were a time in which earlier wishes (partly fulfilled) for social stability and a private, individual perspective can be, and are, taken up once again.

SUGGESTIONS FOR FURTHER READING

William Sheridan Allen, *The Nazi Seizure of Power. The Experience of a Single German Town* (revised edition, London, 1984).

Pierre Aycoberry, *The Nazi Question* (London, 1983).

Omer Bartov, *The Eastern Front, 1941–45, German Troops and the Barbarisation of Warfare* (London, 1986).

Richard Bessel and E. J. Feuchtwanger (eds.), *Social Change and Political Development in Weimar Germany* (London, 1981).

Richard Bessel, *Political Violence and the Rise of Nazism* (New Haven and London, 1984).

Renate Bridenthal et al. (eds.), *When Biology Became Destiny: Women in Weimar and Nazi Germany* (New York, 1984).

Karl Dietrich Bracher, *The German Dictatorship. The Origins, Structure and Effects of National Socialism* (Harmondsworth, 1973).

Martin Broszat, *The Hitler State. The Foundation and Development of the Internal Structure of the Third Reich* (London, 1981).

Hedley Bull (ed.), *The Challenge of the Third Reich* (Oxford, 1986).

William Carr, *Arms, Autarky and Aggression. A Study in German Foreign Policy* (London, 1973).

William Carr, *Hitler. A Study in Personality and Politics* (London, 1978).

Thomas Childers, *The Nazi Voter. The Social Foundations of Fascism in Germany, 1919–1933* (Chapel Hill and London, 1983).

Thomas Childers (ed.), *The Formation of the Nazi Constituency 1918–1933* (London, 1986).

Wilhelm Deist, *The Wehrmacht and German Rearmament* (London, 1982).

Wilhelm Deist (ed.), *The German Military in the Age of Total War* (Leamington Spa, 1985).

Richard J. Evans and Dick Geary (eds.), *The German Unemployed 1918–1936* (London, 1987).

J. E. Farquharson, *The Plough and the Swastika. The NSDAP and Agriculture in Germany 1928–45* (London and Beverley Hills, 1976).

Conan Fischer, *Stormtroopers. A Social, Economic and Ideological Analysis 1929–35* (London, 1983).

Richard Grunberger, *A Social History of the Third Reich* (Harmondsworth, 1974).

John Hiden and John Farquharson, *Explaining Hitler's Germany. Historians and the Third Reich* (London, 1983).

Klaus Hildebrand, *The Foreign Policy of the Third Reich* (London, 1973).

Klaus Hildebrand, *The Third Reich* (London, 1984).

Gerhard Hirschfeld (ed.), *The Politics of Genocide. Jews and Soviet Prisoners of War in Nazi Germany* (London, 1986).

Gerhard Hirschfeld and Lothar Kettenacker (eds.), *Der "Führerstaat": Mythos und Realität* (Stuttgart, 1981) (important articles in English).

Michael Kater, *The Nazi Party. A Social Profile of Members and Leaders, 1919–1945* (Oxford, 1983).

Ian Kershaw, 'The Persecution of the Jews and German Popular Opinion in the Third Reich', in *Leo Baeck Year Book*, xxvi (1981).

Ian Kershaw, *Popular Opinion and Political Dissent in the Third Reich. Bavaria 1933–1945* (Oxford, 1983).

Ian Kershaw, *The Nazi Dictatorship. Problems and Perspectives of Interpretation* (London, 1985).

H. W. Koch (ed.), *Aspects of the Third Reich* (London, 1985).

Helmut Krausnick et al., *Anatomy of the SS State* (London, 1968).

Walter Laqueur (ed.), *Fascism. A Reader's Guide* (Harmondsworth, 1979).

Tim Mason, 'Women in Germany, 1925–1940: Family, Welfare and Work', in *History Workshop Journal*, nos. 1 and 2 (1976).

Tim Mason, 'The Workers' Opposition in Nazi Germany', in *History Workshop Journal*, no. 11 (1981).

Erich Matthias and Anthony Nicholls (eds.), *German Democracy and the Triumph of Hitler* (London, 1971).

Allan Merson, *Communist Resistance in Nazi Germany* (London, 1985).

Franz Neumann, *Behemoth. The Structure and Practice of National Socialism 1933–1944* (New York, 1944).

Jeremy Noakes (ed.), *Government, Party and People in Nazi Germany* (Exeter, 1980).

Jeremy Noakes and Geoffrey Pridham (eds.), *Nazism. 1919–1945. A Documentary Reader* (Exeter, 1984).

R. J. Overy, *The Nazi Economic Recovery 1932–1938* (London, 1982).

Detlev Peukert, *Inside Nazi Germany. Conformity and Opposition in Everyday Life* (London, 1987).

Karl A. Schleunes, *The Twisted Road to Auschwitz. Nazi Policy towards German Jews 1933–1939* (Chicago, 1970).

David Schoenbaum, *Hitler's Social Revolution* (Garden City, N.Y., 1966).

Peter D. Stachura (ed.), *The Shaping of the Nazi State* (London, 1978).

Peter D. Stachura (ed.), *The Nazi Machtergreifung* (London, 1983).

Marlis Steinert, *Hitler's War and the Germans* (Athens, Ohio, 1977).

Jill Stephenson, *Women in Nazi Germany* (London, 1975).

Henry A. Turner (ed.), *Nazism and the Third Reich* (New York, 1972).

Henry A. Turner, *German Big Business and the Rise of Hitler* (New York and Oxford, 1985).

David Welch (ed.), *Nazi Propaganda. The Power and the Limitations* (London, 1983).

NOTES ON CONTRIBUTORS

RICHARD BESSEL is a Lecturer in History at the Open University. He is the author of *Political Violence and the Rise of Nazism* (New Haven and London, 1984) and co-editor (with E. J. Feuchtwanger) of *Social Change and Political Development in Weimar Germany* (London, 1981).

WILLIAM CARR is Professor of Modern History at the University of Sheffield. His books include *Arms, Autarky and Aggression. A Study in German Foreign Policy, 1933–1939* (London, 1972), and *Hitler: A Study of Personality in Politics* (London, 1978).

MICHAEL GEYER is Professor of History at the University of Chicago. His publications include *Aufrüstung oder Sicherheit. Reichswehr in der Krise der Machtpolitik* (Wiesbaden, 1980), and *Deutsche Rüstungspolitik 1860–1980* (Frankfurt/Main, 1984).

ULRICH HERBERT is Hochschulassistent für Neuere Geschichte at the FernUniversität in Hagen. He is the author of *Fremdarbeiter. Politik und Praxis des "Ausländer-Einsatzes" in der Kriegswirtschaft des Dritten Reiches* (Bonn, 1985), and *Geschichte der Ausländerbeschäftigung in Deutschland 1880 bis 1980* (Bonn, 1986).

IAN KERSHAW is a Senior Lecturer in Modern History at the University of Manchester. His books include *Der Hitler-Mythos. Volksmeinung und Propaganda im Dritten Reich* (Stuttgart, 1980), *Popular Opinion and Political Dissent in the Third Reich. Bavaria 1933–1945* (Oxford, 1983), and *The Nazi Dictatorship. Problems and Perspectives of Interpretation* (London, 1985).

JEREMY NOAKES is a Reader in History at the University of Exeter. He is the author of *The Nazi Party in Lower Saxony 1921–1933* (Oxford, 1971), and co-editor (with Geoffrey Pridham) of *Nazism 1919–1945. A Documentary Reader* (2 vols., Exeter, 1983 and 1984).

DETLEV PEUKERT is Privatdozent at the University of Essen. His books include *Die KPD im Widerstand. Verfolgung und Unter-grundarbeit an Rhein und Ruhr 1933 bis 1945* (Wuppertal, 1980), *Grenzen der Sozialdisziplinierung. Aufstieg und Krise der deutschen Jugendfürsorge von 1878 bis 1932* (Cologne, 1986), and *Inside Nazi Germany. Conformity and Opposition in Everyday Life* (London, 1987).

GERHARD WILKE is a Lecturer in Sociology and Social Work at Kingsway College, London, and is the author of numerous articles on village life in nineteenth- and twentieth-century Germany.

INDEX